CW00523401

TORAH -OBSERVANCE

IN

THE AGE OF GRACE

TORAH-OBSERVANCE

IN THE AGE OF GRACE

(What is the place of the

Mosaic Covenant in the age of

the New Covenant?)

by

Bryan W. Sheldon

TORAH-OBSERVANCE IN THE AGE OF GRACE

©   B.W. SHELDON (2016)

All rights reserved

Unless otherwise indicated all Scripture quotations are from the
ESVUK® Bible (The Holy Bible, English Standard Version®),
copyright © 2001 by Crossway, a publishing ministry of Good News
Publishers. Used by permission. All rights reserved.

Scripture quotations taken from the New American Standard Bible®,
Copyright © 1960, 1962, 1963, 1968, 1971, 1972, 1973, 1975, 1977,
1995 by The Lockman Foundation Used by permission.
(www.Lockman.org)

Scripture taken from the New King James Version. Copyright © 1982
by Thomas Nelson, Inc. Used by permission. All rights reserved.

Regarding Scripture quotations from The Authorized (King James)
Version. Rights in the Authorized Version in the United Kingdom are
vested in the Crown. Reproduced by permission of the Crown's
patentee, Cambridge University Press.

Contents

Acknowledgements

As always I acknowledge the debt I owe to those that have gone before. We all stand on the shoulders of previous generations. However, I wish to make special mention of the contribution that my friend and colleague Eddie Donald has made to this subject. His friendship, his Biblical scholarship and his wise advice are greatly valued.

INTRODUCTION

What is the place of the Mosaic Covenant (often referred to as 'the law of Moses')[1] in the age of the New Covenant? There are many that recognize the importance of the ritual of Israel and the contribution that it made to the education of the Hebrew nation - how it was designed to prepare them for the coming of their Messiah. His coming should have changed everything for them. Paul put it well: *"But when the fullness of time had come, God sent forth his Son, born of woman, born under the law, to redeem those who were under the law"* (Gal. 4:4–5). Jesus was born under the law and fulfilled the law, that those under the law might be redeemed. Redeem here means 'to buy out from under the curse and yoke of the law'. Having been redeemed they would no longer be subject to the law. They would have entered into that condition of grace that the Church now enjoys. Sin would no longer have dominion over them for they would no longer be under law but under grace (Rom. 6:14). Alas they rejected their Messiah and the whole situation became more complicated. After the crucifixion of the Lord Jesus, they continued to offer sacrifices in the Temple although the ultimate sacrifice to which those offerings pointed had already been made. The Spring Feasts, that continued to be celebrated, no longer had a future fulfilment. Jesus, the Lamb of God, had died at Passover, been buried at the Feast of Unleavened Bread, and risen at the Feast of Firstfruits; and the Spirit of God had taken up residence in believers at the Feast of Weeks. That God had finished with the ritual of Israel and dismissed the priesthood of Aaron was clearly stated by Jesus when He left the Temple for the last time before His trials. He said, *"See, your house is left to you desolate"* (Matt. 23:38). In the Olivet discourse He told His disciples that God was going to permit the destruction

---

[1] 'Law' in this study refers to the covenant that Israel promised to obey at Sinai. In the New Testament there are other references which point to that 'law' that the conscience is aware of, but in this study we have confined ourselves to what is referred to as 'the law of Moses' (cf. Lk. 2:22; 24:44; John 7:23; Acts 15:5; 1 Cor. 9:9, et al).

of the Temple (Matt. 24:2). This prophecy was fulfilled in A.D. 70 when the army of Titus over-ran the Temple mount and set the sacred buildings on fire. The Jewish Sanctuary, along with its attendant buildings, magnificent porches and gates, was destroyed. The precious furniture from the Holy Place was taken as spoils of war. The troops of Rome had razed Herod's Temple to the ground. The heart of the Israel's legal system of worship had been torn out. The Temple ritual had come to an abrupt end and the Aaronic priesthood ceased to function since it had no place to operate. The whole event added emphasis to the fresh means of grace that had already been provided for the new dispensation. There was now a new way to worship and a new method of approach to God. Jesus had declared as much to a Samaritan woman, *"Jesus said to her, "Woman, believe me, the hour is coming when neither on this mountain nor in Jerusalem will you worship the Father ... But the hour is coming, and is now here, when the true worshipers will worship the Father in spirit and truth, for the Father is seeking such people to worship him"* (John 4:21, 23). In this new period of grace, worshippers would worship in every place *"in spirit and truth"*, coming to the *"throne of grace"*[2] with no other intermediary but Christ. The superior sacrifice of Christ had been offered in a superior sanctuary, a heavenly sanctuary, and this had replaced the Jerusalem Temple. The Aaronic High Priest had been replaced by the High Priest of the Order of Melchizedek, and the sons of Aaron had been replaced by 'the sons of God', that is, those who had embraced the forgiveness provided by the sacrifice of Christ. The festival calendar had been succeeded by a single feast that could be celebrated in any place at any time, with just bread and wine.

But the desire for ritual is strong. Christianity is peppered with groups who have sought to continue (with some adjustment) the mode of worship that Israel used. The Roman Catholic Church has the equivalent of the Jewish High Priest, dressed in special robes, residing in a magnificent building in Rome, somewhat similar to the Temple in Jerusalem. All Catholic Churches have altars at which only those priests ordained by the Roman Catholic Church are allowed to officiate. It is there they offer a sacrifice (the host)

---

[2] Heb. 4:16

which they teach is a re-sacrifice of Christ. They also maintain a division between the priestly caste and the laity which is as clear as it was with only Aaronic priests being allowed in the Holy Place. This pattern is seen in other groups also. The Church of England with its Archbishop, and Bishops, and priestly structure, operates in mighty Cathedrals loosely modelled on the Jewish Temple. Every parish church contains an altar and is built to maintain the separation of clergy and laity. But all this is folly. They have no sacrifice to offer – it has already been offered *"once for all"* (Heb. 7:27). There is only one High Priest, that is, the One who is Head of the Church, Jesus Christ. Those priests who love to be called Father are in direct contradiction to Scripture (cf. Matt. 23:9). Examples could be furnished almost ad-infinitum. It seems this disease – the looking back to the Old Testament dispensation when fulfilling the will of God was more visible – has now been caught by some among the Messianic community and even among some Gentile believers who treasure the Jewishness of Christianity. They are drawn to the old rituals. They recognize they cannot perform them as they should – nevertheless they would like to be able to celebrate the Passover once a year and build booths for the festival of Tabernacles. In the light of Scripture how is this to be viewed? This enquiry, of course, is not whether Jews should abandon their culture, just that, should the rituals prescribed in the Torah still be practiced.

It is not as if this question is not Scriptural: It was faced head on by Paul, an apostle and theologian, who was trained in the Rabbinic schools as well as being divinely instructed. The subject was also debated at length in the early Church – indeed we have the result of their deliberations recorded for us. In addition, we have a letter (Hebrews) which is addressed directly to Jewish Christians with clear advice as to the place of Mosaic ritual in this day of grace. Moreover, Paul, the Jerusalem Council and the writer to the Hebrew believers dealt with the subject while the Temple was still standing, and so did not have the additional difficulties that would be faced by those who wish to celebrate the Feasts today.

What we are suggesting is that, as always, the Bible can give us the answer.

The questions raised could be summarized thus:

1. Do you need to be a Jew to become a Christian?

2. If you are a Christian how do you relate to the law of Moses?

3. Is obedience to the law of Moses still required of members of the Jewish race?

Let us see if we have Scriptural warrant for the stance we have already taken in this introduction. These are the questions to be considered as we travel through some pertinent passages.

CHAPTER ONE

LIGHT FROM THE LETTER TO THE GALATIANS

Let's first consider how Paul handled the subjects in his letter to the Galatians. If an early date for its writing is accepted, then it precedes the debate in Jerusalem which is reported by Luke in Acts 15. After offering a greeting of grace and peace, Paul quickly addresses the problem. It seems some of the Judaizing party had already visited Galatia in his absence and called on the Gentile believers there to submit to the law, in order to have access to the benefits of the death of Christ.[3] Paul identified this approach as a distortion of the gospel of Christ. *"I am astonished that you are so quickly deserting him who called you in the grace of Christ and are turning to a different gospel—not that there is another one, but there are some who trouble you and want to distort the gospel of Christ"* (Gal. 1:6–7). He is so outraged that he is prepared to declare any who preach the necessity of law to supplement grace 'anathema', that is, 'cursed'; no matter what credentials they claimed. *"But even if we or an angel from heaven should preach to you a gospel contrary to the one we preached to you, let him be accursed. As we have said before, so now I say again: If anyone is preaching to you a gospel contrary to the one you received, let him be accursed"* (Gal. 1:8–9). His reason for such strong language is because it seeks to undermine the truth communicated to him from Christ Himself. *"For I would have you know, brothers, that the gospel that was preached by me is not man's gospel. For I did not receive it from any man, nor was I taught it, but I received it through a revelation of Jesus Christ"* (Gal. 1:11–12). The gospel he preached did not envisage a saving quality in the law, indeed the emphasis was *'not a result of works'* (Eph. 2:9). Furthermore, since he is writing to those who have already responded to the gospel of grace and been saved, we can confidently infer that he is also saying that the law adds nothing to the Christian experience. Not only is 'the gospel of grace' the door by which you enter the family of God, it is also the gospel by which you live once you are saved.

---

[3] Acts 15:1

10

We are saved by grace[4], we continue in the grace of God,[5] and we grow in grace.[6] Anything that takes you in the direction of works subsequent to salvation is also a perversion of the gospel. *"I am astonished that you are so quickly deserting him who called you in the grace of Christ and are turning to a different gospel"* (Gal. 1:6).[7] In Paul's theology, the law and its works are intimately connected to the flesh (as we shall see later) and should not be part of the believer's experience.

Paul goes on to support the integrity of his apostleship and the law-free gospel he received from Jesus Christ, by recounting a previous meeting he had with the leaders of the Jerusalem church. The issue of circumcision, which was central to the message brought by those of the Judaizing party, had surfaced and been rejected at this earlier visit to Jerusalem when Paul was accompanied by Titus, a Gentile believer whom Paul refused to have circumcised despite pressure from certain *"false brothers"* (Gal. 2:3-4).

The issue of circumcision is of supreme importance since it was considered the rite of entry into the privileges and responsibilities of the people of God (Lev. 12:3). The significance of circumcision was impressed on Moses when he nearly lost his life at the hand of God because his son was uncircumcised (Exod. 4:24–26). The next generation of Israelites were also made aware of the importance of this rite of initiation for they were forbidden to enter the Promised Land without it (Josh. 5:1–9). But Paul teaches that circumcision is no longer necessary to belong to the redeemed people of God (Gal. 5:2–4, 6; 6:15). It is no longer the rite of entry into the family of God. Those, who in this age of grace rely simply on their Jewish pedigree are facing major disappointment and eternal sorrow. Moreover, those who seek to observe the law subsequent to salvation also are on a path that will lead to shipwreck. Paul writes: *"Look: I, Paul, say to you that if you accept circumcision, Christ will be of no advantage to you. I testify again to every*

---

[4] Eph. 2:5
[5] Acts 13:43
[6] 2 Pet. 3:18
[7] Emphasis added by the author. This applies throughout the book.

man who accepts circumcision that he is obligated to keep the whole law. You are severed from Christ, you who would be justified by the law; you have fallen away from grace" (Gal. 5:2–4). In using the phrase *"fallen away from grace"*, I would suggest that Paul is not here referring to losing salvation (that is eternally secure) – but rather losing the benefit of living the Christian life under the regime of grace and losing sweet fellowship with the *"God of all grace"* (1 Pet.5:10). Obviously, the Judaizers did not for a moment believe that the imposition of circumcision involved alienation from Christ. But they did consider it a necessary requirement for the true possession of salvation. What they advocated was a mingling of the grace of Christ with the merit of works. But law and grace are mutually exclusive. Those that take on works to demonstrate devotion to God are placing themselves under the necessity to fulfil the whole law. This negates the value of the death of Christ for them, since Jesus died to free us from the law.

Paul argues that the initiation rite into the Mosaic covenant is no longer required. This in turn means that the covenant itself is no longer operative. It must be underlined that this does not remove the requirement for Jewish males to be circumcised. That remains in place as part of the Abrahamic Covenant and is not under scrutiny here. The Abrahamic Covenant is eternal and unconditional whereas the Mosaic Covenant was temporary and conditional[8] and at present we are only concerned with the Mosaic Covenant. Paul asserts that between himself and the Jerusalem leaders there was solidarity and a common front in the work of the gospel, for they saw "*that I had been entrusted with the gospel to the uncircumcised, just as Peter had been entrusted with the gospel to the circumcised*" (Gal. 2:7).

PAUL'S REBUKE OF PETER

Some that wished to retain the Jewishness of the gospel to such a degree that they would make salvation dependent on candidates acknowledging the authority of the law of Moses and be Torah observant had also visited

---

[8] See my book 'The Messiah and the Covenants of Israel' (Port Colborne, Gospel Folio Press, 2009)

Antioch. They taught, *"Unless you are circumcised according to the custom of Moses, you cannot be saved"* (Acts 15:1). It may be that these are the ones identified as *"false brothers"* in Gal.2:4 *"who slipped in to spy out our freedom that we have in Christ Jesus, so that they might bring us into slavery"*.[9] If so, it certainly casts light upon Paul's rebuke of Peter recounted later in the same chapter. *"But when Cephas came to Antioch, I opposed him to his face, because he stood condemned. For before certain men came from James, he was eating with the Gentiles; but when they came he drew back and separated himself, fearing the circumcision party. And the rest of the Jews acted hypocritically along with him, so that even Barnabas was led astray by their hypocrisy. But when I saw that their conduct was not in step with the truth of the gospel, I said to Cephas before them all, "If you, though a Jew, live like a Gentile and not like a Jew, how can you force the Gentiles to live like Jews?"'"* (Gal. 2:11–14) While Peter did not wish to alienate the Jews from Jerusalem, Paul was able to see the importance of the issue and make a stand. It was not just on the principle that salvation was on the basis of faith in the death of Christ only, not the death of Christ plus Torah observance; it was also to deal with Torah observance after justification. Peter's salvation was not in doubt, but his relapse back into observing the rule of law after salvation was not only not wise, but also undermined the double truth, that both justification and the subsequent Christian life were totally dependent on the grace of God. Paul addresses both matters in this letter.

Regarding justification, he wrote: *"we ourselves are Jews by birth and not Gentile sinners; yet we know that **a person is not justified by works of the law** but through faith in Jesus Christ, so we also have believed in Christ Jesus, in order to be justified by faith in Christ and not by works of the law, because **by works of the law no one will be justified**"* (Gal. 2:15–16).

---

[9] Note how Paul equates 'under grace' to freedom; 'under law' to slavery (see also chapter 4; allegory 2).

Regarding our walk, he wrote: *"But I say, walk by the Spirit, and you will not gratify the desires of the flesh. For the desires of the flesh are against the Spirit, and the desires of the Spirit are against the flesh, for these are opposed to each other, to keep you from doing the things you want to do. But if you are led by the Spirit, **you are not under the law**"* (Gal. 5:16–18).

Paul would pronounce 'anathema' on any that preached that salvation was obtained in any way other than that of faith in the sacrifice of Christ. Indeed, he took it further – he (previously a champion of the law) maintained that if he returned to any level of Torah observance for any aspect of righteousness it would be sin. *"For if I rebuild what I have once destroyed, I prove myself to be a transgressor"* (Gal. 2:18). He said that being dead to the law was the only way to enjoy the life of Christ. *"For through the law **I died to the law, so that I might live to God**. I have been crucified with Christ. It is no longer I who live, but Christ who lives in me. And the life I now live in the flesh I live by faith in the Son of God, who loved me and gave himself for me"* (Gal. 2:19–20).

His language is very strong: *"**For all who rely on works of the law are under a curse**; for it is written, "Cursed be everyone who does not abide by all things written in the Book of the Law, and do them""* (Gal. 3:10, Quoted from Deut. 27:26). Not only is the language strong, it is also unambiguous: *"the law is not of faith"* (Gal. 3:12); and since *"the righteous shall live by faith"* (Gal. 3:11), going back to Torah observance is immature. The age of law was when Israel was young and under a tutor; the age of grace is the age of maturity when childish habits should be left behind. *"When I was a child, I spoke like a child, I thought like a child, I reasoned like a child. When I became a man, I gave up childish ways"* (1 Cor. 13:11).

So what was the main purpose of the law and when would it cease? Paul asks and answers these very questions: *"Why then the law? It was added because of transgressions, **until the offspring should come** to whom the promise had been made"* (Gal. 3:19). It was added ... *"because of transgressions"*, that is, to provide a temporary covering for sin; *"until the offspring"* (that is the 'seed of the woman', Christ) should come. Christ has come and the age of law is over! The Bible is very clear – the age of law has been superseded by the age of grace, and the instrument of covenant on which this age is founded is simply called the New Covenant.

So, for those who have put their faith in a crucified Messiah, the curse of the law has been negated by the death of Christ on Golgotha. Anne Ross Cousin wrote:

Death and the curse were in our cup,

O Christ, 'twas full for Thee!

But Thou hast drained the last dark drop,

'Tis empty now for me.

The bitter cup, love drank it up;

Now blessings' draught for me.

The implication is that Christ, in taking upon Himself our sins, also took upon Himself the curse of the law. *"Christ redeemed us from the curse of the law **by becoming a curse for us**—for it is written, "Cursed is everyone who is hanged on a tree"— **so that in Christ Jesus the blessing of Abraham might come to the Gentiles,** so that we might receive the promised Spirit through faith"* (Gal. 3:13–14). Here then is introduced an amazing concept – that Gentiles now have access to the Abrahamic Covenant (at least that which provides blessing to those who have the faith of Abraham and can be called the *"sons of Abraham"* (Gal. 3:7)). **The Mosaic Covenant (the law) which excluded the Gentiles has been removed** (Eph. 2:14–15).

THE CURSE OF THE LAW?

The Torah is very clear – obey and be blessed – disobey and be cursed. Moses spoke to the assembled nation prior to their entry into the Promised Land: *"See, I am setting before you today a blessing and a curse: the blessing, if you obey the commandments of the LORD your God, which I command you today, and the curse, if you do not obey the commandments of the LORD your God"* (Deut. 11:26–28). Since the Bible declares that those of Jewish descent have been guilty of disobedience (just like all others), then it is clear that the law could not provide a permanent solution for their difficulty. The rejection and crucifixion of their Messiah was perhaps the single, clearest piece of evidence that they are law-breakers who need some mighty act of grace to answer their predicament. Paradoxically, the death of the Messiah by crucifixion was that very act of grace, when He voluntarily took upon Himself the curse that was directed to those that disobey the law. This was accomplished when He placed Himself in harm's way to be betrayed by one of His disciples, before being illegally tried by a prejudiced court and handed to the Gentiles for execution. He was nailed to a cross – a form of punishment deliberately designed as an offence to the Jewish people but embraced by the Messiah to facilitate the offer of salvation to the Hebrew nation. Although this radical act carried with it a consequence which initially looked as if it would be a hindrance to Jews, nevertheless it was designed to lead to an offer of salvation which included freedom from the Sinai code which only condemned them. Notwithstanding the benefits that issue from the death of Christ, many of those that have spent their lives under the canopy of the Mosaic economy fail to respond to the preaching of the cross. For them it remains a *"stumbling block"* (1 Cor. 1:23).

THE CROSS A STUMBLING BLOCK?

Let us expand this a little. A crucified Messiah is a stumbling block to the Jews because the mode of execution made the individual accursed. The Torah states: *"his body shall not remain all night on the tree, but you shall bury him the same day, for a hanged man is cursed by God"* (Deut. 21:23). This refers to one of the forms of Jewish execution, hanging; but Paul sees it as applicable also to crucifixion. So, here then is the 'offence of the cross' (as it is termed in the KJV), as far as a Jew is concerned. They have strong objections to a Messiah who was cursed. Paul would have been aware of this Scripture. Prior to his Damascus Road experience, he considered those who maintained that a crucified Jesus was the Messiah were guilty of blasphemy and should be punished. He – a Hebrew of Hebrews – volunteered to be the one to deal with this outrageous new sect. But a meeting with the exalted Christ put an end to that! Nevertheless, the difficulty remained. A crucified Messiah was an anathema to the Jews. The explanation, as we have already identified, is that all members of the Hebrew race are under the curse because of their inability to keep the law. *"For **all who rely on works of the law are under a curse;** for it is written, "Cursed be everyone who does not abide by all things written in the Book of the law, and do them"* (Gal. 3:10). The curse of the law is clearly defined in Deuteronomy 28. but see also Leviticus 26:

"But if you will not obey the voice of the LORD your God or be careful to do all his commandments and his statutes that I command you today, then all these curses shall come upon you and overtake you.

Cursed shall you be in the city, and cursed shall you be in the field.

Cursed shall be your basket and your kneading bowl.

Cursed shall be the fruit of your womb and the fruit of your ground, the increase of your herds and the young of your flock.

Cursed shall you be when you come in, and cursed shall you be when you go out" (Deut. 28:15–19).

This chapter goes on to list diseases of body and mind that could cling to those that obdurately refused to honour the law (vv.21, 22, 27, 28, 35, 59-61). From these passages arose the practice of giving up such offenders to a 'cherem' or curse. The Jews expressed it as giving them up to Satan. Obdurate law-breakers would lose the protection that God provides for His people. They would, like Job, be exposed to the activity of Satan - and could suffer a similar fate to Job. An offender who resisted correction and exhausted all remedy contained in the law would become 'a curse among his people'. The Messiah remarked on such a one, a woman who was bent over and unable to stand straight: *"And this woman, a daughter of Abraham as she is, whom Satan has bound for eighteen long years, should she not have been released from this bond on the Sabbath day?"* (Luke 13:16) Another was the paralytic dropped at the feet of Jesus recorded in Matthew 9; Mark 2 and Luke 5. To the paralytic Jesus first said, *"Take courage, son; your sins are forgiven"* (Matt.9:2).

In forgiving their sins, healing their bodies and delivering them from Satan, Jesus was clearly anticipating the full benefit of His sacrificial death. This multi-layered act of redemption can only be explained by the fact that, among other things, they were delivered from the curse of the law.

But what happened at Calvary to make this sophisticated act of redemption possible? How were they, and indeed all believers, delivered from the curse of the law? By the act of substitution. Christ was pronounced 'cherem' instead of us. Paul writes, *"Christ redeemed **us** from the curse of the law by becoming a curse **for us**—for it is written, "Cursed is everyone who is hanged on a tree"* (Gal. 3:13).

THE CRUCIFIED CHRIST DEALS WITH THE CURSE OF THE LAW.

Here then, is one reason, why the death of the Messiah had to be by crucifixion. A 'cursed' Messiah, might be despised by the Jewish people, but nevertheless was absolutely necessary for them. The Jewish people were under the 'curse of the law' because they could not keep it. R. Levi said, if they could only keep the Sabbath fully for one day, then Messiah would come[10]. But they could not even keep one Sabbath perfectly. Nevertheless, they were saved from the wrath of God because He had given them a remedy in the sacrificial system.

But why deal with this subject in a letter to Gentiles? Because the Galatians were being enticed to enter the Church through the door of the Mosaic covenant. The Judaizers expected them to be circumcised, observe the feasts and holy days in the Mosaic calendar, indeed obey the whole law. Paul was very clear. He said that returning to the Mosaic covenant only led to bondage, the curse and death. *"For all who rely on works of the law are under a curse; for it is written, "Cursed be everyone who does not abide by all things written in the Book of the Law, and do them"* (Gal. 3:10 cf. Deut.27.26).

---

[10] Midrash Rabbah on Ps.95.7

The main inference to be drawn from this Scripture is that you cannot cherry-pick which parts of the Torah to obey – it is all or nothing – *"Cursed be everyone who does not abide **by all things written in the Book of the Law, and do them**"* (Gal. 3:10). James makes the same point: *"For whoever keeps the whole law but fails in one point has become accountable for all of it"* (James 2:10).

Not only so, but notice how the law and the curse are inextricably linked – *"all who rely on works of the law are under a curse"*. Adam was given one law to obey – he failed and the curse has affected everyone ever since. For to those who wish to observe the Torah, even to a limited degree, (which we have already noted is not possible) we ask, 'why put yourself in danger by playing (yes – that's the right word) at Torah-observance when all evidence says it will backfire resulting in grief and loss?

CHAPTER TWO

THE JERUSALEM COUNCIL

The influence of Jewish Christians who wished to impose conditions on the entrance of the Gentiles into the Church was of such importance that eventually it was necessary to bring the matter to James and other of the Apostles in Jerusalem, especially since some of the Judaizers claimed to have the authority of James for their doctrine. Paul and Barnabas led the delegation and were warmly welcomed by the Jerusalem church and its leaders. Many rejoiced in the news that a large number of Gentiles had believed and embraced the gospel of grace.

However, there were still those among the Jewish Christians who had serious reservations about the way the outreach to Gentiles had been conducted. The more conservative Jewish Christians felt that they should be received on the same basis that Jews had always accepted Gentiles into the covenant community—through proselyte initiation. This involved circumcision of the males and all proselytes taking upon themselves the total provisions of the Mosaic law. For all intents and purposes, a Gentile proselyte to Judaism became a Jew, not only in religious conviction but in lifestyle as well. This became the main topic of discussion. The leading speakers in the forum were Peter, Paul, Barnabas and finally James, the half-brother of the Messiah and the leader of the Jerusalem Church.

PETER'S CONTRIBUTION

Peter, who still held the authority of Apostle to the Jews, gave testimony to the event that changed his mind-set, that of the conversion of Cornelius and his household (Acts 10). He contended that God, who knows the hearts of men, by a mighty demonstration of the Spirit, received and cleansed this group of Gentiles from their sins without requiring them to embrace the sign of the Abrahamic covenant or become subject to the Mosaic covenant. They only had to meet the one condition, that of faith. Peter makes explicit that which was implicit in the conversion of Cornelius. "*And God, who knows the heart, bore witness to them, by giving them the Holy Spirit just as he did to us, and he made no distinction between us and them, having cleansed their hearts by faith"* (Acts 15:8–9). His advice was - do not put God to the test by adding conditions to the basic requirement that God has evidently established – that all, Jew and Gentile, must be saved by grace alone, through faith alone, in Christ alone. His description of the law, which was the requirement advocated by the Pharisaic party, is interesting; it is **"a yoke ... that neither our fathers nor we have been able to bear?"** (Acts 15:10)

JAMES' JUDGEMENT

After Paul and Barnabas shared their missionary experiences, James, a pillar of the church in Jerusalem, rose to speak. He began by referring to Peter's testimony of God's acceptance of the Gentiles at Cornelius's home and said, God *"visited the Gentiles, to take from them a people for his name"* (Acts 15:14). James used the word *'laos'* to describe the Gentiles, a term usually applied to Israel. In Zechariah 2:11, the Septuagint applies the term *'laos'* to the Gentiles also, who will in the final days come to dwell in the renewed Zion and be a part of God's people. Something like this seems to be the meaning here. In Christ, God brings Jew and Gentile together into a single *'laos'*, a single people *"for His name"*. James then showed how the coming of the Gentiles was in accordance with the purposes of God. He referenced Amos 9:11–12. *"And with this the words of the prophets agree, just as it is written, "'After this I will return, and I will rebuild the tent of David that has fallen; I will rebuild its ruins, and I will restore it, that the remnant of mankind may seek the Lord, and all the Gentiles who are called by my name, says the Lord, who makes these things known from of old"'* (Acts 15:15–18). Since the T'nach confirms that God's purposes include the Gentiles, and Peter's testimony says it began with Cornelius on the basis of faith alone, it is evident that the conversion of the Gentiles did not then, and does not now, require them to enter the 'ekklesia' through the doorway of the law. James, speaking as leader of the Jerusalem church and the assembled council pronounced their decision - *"Therefore my judgment is that we should not trouble those of the Gentiles who turn to God, but should write to them to abstain from the things polluted by idols, and from sexual immorality, and from what has been strangled, and from blood"* (Acts 15:19–20). The prohibitions that James enumerated were really not something radically new. They are found in Lev 17 and 18 as requirements expected of resident aliens.[11] Perhaps this is what James meant in his rather obscure concluding remark in verse 21: *"For from ancient generations Moses has had in every city those who proclaim him, for he is read every Sabbath in the synagogues."* In other words, these requirements should come as no surprise to the Gentiles. They have been required of Gentiles associating with Jews from the earliest times. But James's remark could also be taken in another sense, which would fit the context well: there are Jews in every city who cherish the Torah. Gentile Christians should be sensitive to their scruples and not give them offence in these matters, for they too may be reached with the gospel.

This judgement, releasing Gentiles from Torah-observance, was sent by messengers to Antioch before gradually disseminating throughout the churches bringing joy and encouragement to all Gentile converts.

While the initial debate was designed to deal only with the rules of reception of Gentiles into the community of believers, the judgement proved to have a much wider application impacting as it does on their practice of the faith.

---

[11] Lev. 17:8; 13, 10-14; 18:6-23

CHAPTER THREE

LIGHT FROM THE ROMAN LETTER

There are two major theological treatises in the New Testament: Romans and Hebrews. In Paul's Roman epistle the cross is still central, but his theology is more sophisticated than in his earlier letters. In it he analyses the problems humankind faces, and seeks to provide the solution. He first demonstrates how the crucified Christ deals with the penalty of sin. The initial problem that everyone has to face is – 'how can we be delivered from the wrath of God, since we all are guilty sinners?' (cf. Rom. 1.18-3.23). The argument is that if the Jews could not keep the law and they had every advantage, there is no way the Gentiles could have escaped the punishment directed at law-breakers. *"Now we know that whatever the law says it speaks to those who are under the law, so that **every mouth may be stopped**, and **the whole world** may be held accountable to God. For by works of the law no human being will be justified in his sight"* (Rom. 3:19,20).

The Apostle says the wrath of God can only be averted by placing your faith in a crucified Messiah. There was a cleansing agent released at Calvary that is powerful enough to wash us clean. It is, of course, the precious blood of Christ: we, *"are justified by his grace as a gift, through the redemption that is in Christ Jesus, whom God put forward as a propitiation **by his blood**, to be received by faith"* (3.24,25).[12] Thus we are delivered from the penalty of sin. Now no more worry – at least about the sin question: For He made *"peace through the blood of His cross"* (Col 1:20).

But our problems are quite complex. What about our propensity to sin? It is not simply that we are sinners because we sin, but also that we sin because we are sinners. The blood can deal with the sins we have committed, but where can we find help to live a holy life?

---

[12] 'Propitiation' is translated 'a sacrifice of atonement' in the NRSV

SOME THOUGHT THE LAW WAS THE ANSWER BUT IT WAS NOT

Paul approaches the subject in the context of the problems he had faced in Christian communities all over Asia Minor. In those churches, in Paul's absence, believers had been told that they should obey the law of Moses. There was a 'back to Moses' campaign being waged by some that claimed their authority from the Jerusalem church (See Gal. 1:6 ff; Acts 15:1). They were declaring that the only entry into the 'ekklesia' was through the door of the Mosaic Covenant, the law. Paul would have none of it—he declared it 'another gospel' and cursed any that preached it (Gal. 1:8). However, Torah-observance was a strong attraction for those who had been brought up under the law, and many wanted to embrace it. The arguments presented in support of the law were powerful. It had been given by God and had helped to govern Israel for millennia. Jesus Himself had been Torah-observant. And remember, the Temple was still standing at the time of the Roman letter. The festivals from Passover to Tabernacles with their attractive rituals were still nationally observed. Even Gentiles felt drawn to life under the canopy of the law of Moses and some Christian leaders like Peter and Barnabas had, for a short while, been pressured into returning to the old life of legal separation (Gal.2:11 ff).

The doctrine that was abroad was very difficult to combat. One form of it was: you are saved by grace but you continue by works. But it was a pernicious doctrine, and Christ's Ambassador was prepared to go to the barricades and take a stand against it. He argued that if no-one could keep the law to be justified, that is, to be saved, there is no way that any could keep the law to maintain their position of acceptance. At the beginning of chapter seven it seems he is addressing the Jews in particular (*"do you not know, brothers—for I am speaking to those who know the law)"* (Rom. 7:1). Nevertheless, his words are fashioned in such a way to be effective for the Gentiles as well. He says no-one can maintain the righteousness they were granted by placing themselves under the law. That is like providing sin with the resources it needs to be master over you. Don't do it: *"do not go on presenting the members of your body to sin as instruments of unrighteousness; but present yourselves to God as those alive from the dead, and your members as instruments of righteousness to God. For sin shall not*

Contact details:

Bryan W. Sheldon
26 Park Drive
Newport,
NP20 3AL

Email: b.sheldon@ntlworld.com

Web: www.bryansbiblestudy.co.uk

Phone: 01633 661579

For those who wish to register, there is a teaching newsletter distributed bi-monthly, free of charge.

If you wish to receive it, it is available as hard copy or by email. Just fill in the appropriate details below (name and address if you would like it by post, or name and email address if you would like it by email).

I would like to receive the teaching newsletter from Mountjoy Ministries.

By post: ☐   By email: ☐   Please tick one

Name: ....

Address ....

....

.........................Post code....................................

Email: ....

Please send to Bryan at the above address.

*be master over you, for **you are not under law but under grace***" (Rom. 6:13–14).

JESUS DIED THAT WE MIGHT LIVE A RIGHTEOUS LIFE

Paul says, go back to Calvary and understand what happened there. The glory of Christ's work on the cross is that He identified Himself with us - He died in our place, as our substitute. So for salvation and much more, we need to identify ourselves with Him. Ah! But that means identifying ourselves with a 'cursed' Messiah. We cannot live for Christ without embracing the offence of the cross. We seek to sanitize Calvary, but it was an horrendous place where Jesus was humiliated – being executed naked as a charlatan, a traitor, a rebel, a blasphemer, a sorcerer, and a fiend. But remember, Jesus took our place on the cross. If our identification with Christ is real and total, we should say. 'I was the charlatan, traitor, rebel, blasphemer, sorcerer, fiend'. This means we will never be able to say, 'I am better than anyone else'. We will always be sinners saved by grace, and at best 'unprofitable servants'.

But this identification with a rejected and despised Messiah has an upside too. Thoreaux said, 'For every thousand hacking at the leaves of sin, there is only one hacking at the roots'. In Romans Paul gives us the truth that will enable us to deal with the roots of sin. It is - our 'old nature', our Adamic nature, our sinful nature, was put to death on the cross: "*We know that our old self was crucified with him in order that the body of sin might be brought to nothing, so that we would no longer be enslaved to sin*" (Rom. 6:6). This is presented by Paul as a truth as important as that which we understood and embraced to be saved. Jesus did not die only to provide eternal life but also to enable individuals to live a life of righteousness. It is presented here as another crisis (calling for action) to be followed by a process. "*Even so **consider** yourselves to be dead to sin, but alive to God in Christ Jesus. Therefore do not let sin reign in your mortal body so that you obey its lusts, and do not go on presenting the members of your body to sin as instruments of unrighteousness; but **present** yourselves to God as those alive from the dead, and your members as instruments of righteousness to God.*" (Rom. 6:11–13).

The word 'consider' in verse 11 (translated 'reckon' in the KJV) introduces a fact that you can count on. Paul advises, 'count on the fact that you are dead to sin but alive to God'. This is the necessary precursor to the commitment that Paul suggests a believer should make; a commitment that is suggested by the word "present" (highlighted in the above text). The word 'present' is an 'aorist, active, imperative' verb. In other words, it calls for an immediate, once and for all, act of dedication. Present yourselves to God, fully, completely, without reserve and with no intention of drawing back. Paul says—do it and do it now! Here is Paul's pathway to a fulfilling Christian life.

1. **Understand,** that is, "knowing this" (6:6), that what happened at Calvary impacted on you. Those that subsequently embrace the sacrifice of Christ for salvation are considered to have been *"united with Christ"* when He died (6:5).

2. **Count (reckon) on it**—it is a fact as strong as any on which you stood to be saved. This will enable you to be 'dead to sin' and 'alive to God'.

3. **Present** yourself to God as those alive from the dead, and your members are instruments of righteousness (6:13).[13]

But it means a constant embracing of the power of Calvary. If we live 'in Christ', if we walk 'in Him', the power of sin is broken. It is negated because that on which it works is dead. But if you walk in the flesh, the power of sin is revived. *"There is therefore now no condemnation for those who are in Christ Jesus. For the law of the Spirit of life has set you free in Christ Jesus from the law of sin and death"* (Rom. 8:1–2).

What is suggested here is, if you return to law-keeping the power of sin is revived. But, say those who wish to honour the law, it is described as *"holy*

---

[13] Watchman Nee famously identified the three stages, 'Know'; Reckon'; and 'Present' in the book 'The Normal Christian Life' published by Victory Press (London) 1961

and righteous and good" (Rom. 7:12). Paul answers this conundrum. Having first asked *"is the law sin"* (Rom. 7:7 NASB) and answered: *"By no means!"* he continues to explain: *"Yet if it had not been for the law, I would not have known sin. For I would not have known what it is to covet if the law had not said, "You shall not covet." But sin, seizing an opportunity through the commandment, produced in me all kinds of covetousness. For apart from the law, sin lies dead"* (Rom. 7:7–8).

Those that wish to keep the law, whatever aspect and to whatever degree have an inadequate understanding of the law and its purpose. Part of its purpose was to make evident the exceeding sinfulness of sin. A sinfulness which left untreated will kill. Paul offered his testimony to elucidate: *"I was once alive apart from the law, but when the commandment came, sin came alive and I died. The very commandment that promised life proved to be death to me. For sin, seizing an opportunity through the commandment, deceived me and through it killed me"* (Rom. 7:9–11). This text illuminates an important principle. **law-keeping is deceptive and injurious**. Those who think keeping the law honours God have been deceived on two counts.

1. They cannot keep the law (even in part it will fall short of the commandment) and
2. It is an affront to the One who gave His Son to deliver us from the bondage the law produces.

The Romans 7:9 text prompts us to ask, when was Paul *"alive apart from the law"*? It could not have been before his conversion because as a Jew born of Jewish parents he was always under the law. This condition only arises after conversion. But it seems that Paul faced the same difficulty that all must face – how do you live a life to please God once you are saved. His initial response (similar to many) was; 'I must now obey the law'. But he (similar to all) found it to be an impossible aim, especially as, after conversion, he did not have the legal remedy available under the Mosaic code, the sacrificial system, to ease his conscience. So when he placed himself under the law sin revived. He said, *"For I do not do the good I want, but the evil I do not want is what I keep on doing"* (Rom. 7:19). Paul has no criticism of the law – in his heart he delights in it.[14] But he is not able to keep it - *"For I know that nothing good dwells in me, that is, in my flesh. For I have the desire to do what is right, but not the ability to carry it out"* (Rom. 7:18). He was in despair: *"Wretched man that I am! Who will set me free from the body of this death?"* (Rom. 7:24) However, his despair was dissipated – he was set free from Torah observance by Christ. *"For the law of the Spirit of life in Christ Jesus has made me free from the law of sin and death"* (Rom.8:2, NKJV). And no law means no condemnation: *"There is therefore now no condemnation for those who are in Christ Jesus"* (Rom. 8:1).

WHAT OF THE LAW NOW?

But does that mean we can ignore the law of God and do what we like? By no means! Those features that especially relate to righteous living included in the Mosaic code have been brought over into the new dispensation of grace. James calls them *"the law of liberty"* (James 1:25; 2:12). Paul calls them the *"the righteous requirement of the law"* (Rom. 8:4). If we walk in the Spirit we are credited with the value of the righteous life of Christ, and in obedience to our conscience will fulfil such aspects of the law that are appropriate for a dispensation of grace. *"For God has done what the law, weakened by the flesh, could not do. By sending his own Son in the likeness of sinful flesh and for sin, he condemned sin in the flesh, in order that **the righteous requirement of the law might be fulfilled in us, who walk** not according to the flesh but **according to the Spirit"** (Rom. 8:3–4).

Failure to keep **the whole law** (which is the requirement) is now no longer a difficulty. In chapter 10 he offers a phrase that declares that righteousness through the law has finished. *"For Christ is the end of the law for righteousness to everyone who believes"* (Rom 10:4).

---

[14] Rom. 7:22

THE DEATH OF THE MESSIAH WAS THE 'END' OF THE LAW

The word *'end'* (τέλος) has been the subject of much debate. Commentaries discuss at length whether 'τέλος' means "end" in the sense of "termination" or in the sense of "goal." Bruce suggests it holds both senses, that is, it means that Christ is the goal of the law "in that he embodies the perfect righteousness which it prescribes," and "this implies the termination of the law's function (real or imagined) as a means of acquiring such a righteous status".[15]

But Paul's affection for his fellow-Jews remained constant, as is recorded at the beginning of Romans 10. *"Brothers, my heart's desire and prayer to God for them* (Israel) *is that they may be saved."* But He points out that their zeal is currently misdirected for they are seeking to gain acceptance with God by self-discipline and obedience instead of trusting in the grace, mercy and love of God. They are looking for salvation by works when it is by grace. *"For I bear them witness that they have a zeal for God, but not according to knowledge. For, being ignorant of the righteousness of God, and seeking to establish their own, they did not submit to God's righteousness. For Christ is the end of the law for righteousness to everyone who believes"* (Rom.10:1–4).

The law cannot now provide a way to arrive at a right standing with God and comes to an end in Christ. It is brought to an end so that righteousness may be within the reach of all who believe. As the hymn writer A. M. Toplady put it, "Nothing in my hand I bring; simply to Thy cross I cling". **The only thing God requires of people is that they not persist in trying to earn what they can only receive as a totally free gift.**

---

[15] Comment on Rom. 10:4: FF Bruce 'The Letter of Paul to the Romans' Wm. B. Eerdmans Publishing, 1985

CHAPTER FOUR

LIGHT FROM THE RABBINIC USE OF ALLEGORY

The biographical details of Paul reveal that he was trained in Rabbinic thought and this is evident by his use of allegory, that is, to speak figuratively to convey deeper truth. There are three particular instances which impact on our subject. In Galatians he speaks of the law as a tutor; and then later in the same letter he allegorises the personal history of Abraham and Sarah and their treatment of Hagar and her son; and in Romans he speaks of the law as a husband with high standards and inflexible demands. We begin this section with a question.

WHAT WAS THE PURPOSE OF THE LAW?

Since there were those in the early Christian community that had diametrically opposing views regarding the role that the law should play, Paul takes time to spell out its purpose. For example, in Romans, the law is described as an instrument to awaken the knowledge of sin; in Ephesians it is described as a "dividing wall" (Eph. 2:14 NASB) to separate Jew and Gentile, but in Galatians he personifies the Mosaic code as a teacher, an instructor, a tutor.

ALLEGORY 1: THE LAW AS A TUTOR

He wrote: "*the law has become our tutor to lead us to Christ, so that we may be justified by faith*" (Gal. 3:24 NASB). The image proposed is of a son in a wealthy family who is under a tutor until he comes to the age of maturity. It is then he takes on the responsibilities and enters into the privileges of sonship. In other words, the Torah and the ritual of Israel were designed to prepare Israel for the coming of their Messiah. If the Jewish people had accepted Jesus, they would have entered into the full privileges and responsibilities of God's first-born (Exod.4:22). Indeed, that seems to have been the first objective of Christ's coming as indicated in Galatians 4:4–5.

Alas, the leadership of the nation rebelled, and demonstrated that they had not embraced the lessons provided. The Sanhedrists with their seats of power did not wish to relinquish their lucrative positions. Jesus implied as much when he pointed a parable in their direction. Casting them in the role of tenants of God's vineyard, He removed any ambiguity by having them state in very clear terms what was in their minds and hearts - *"But when the tenants saw the son, they said to themselves, 'This is the heir.* **Come, let us kill him and have his inheritance** *"* (Matt. 21:38). Yet these were the very ones who projected themselves as patriotic Jews, many putting themselves forward as those who defended not only the Mosaic law but also the extrapolated laws of the teachers. But Jesus pronounced them hypocrites, sons of hell and blind guides (See Matt. 23:13-35).

But God is very gracious. Although nationally, because of the failure of their ruling body, the Jewish nation as a whole did not enter into the blessing that was offered, the grace of God made it possible for individuals to be treated separately. Peter exhorted all who heard him at the Feast of Weeks to disassociate themselves from the national decision taken by the Sanhedrin: He *"continued to exhort them, saying, "Save yourselves from this crooked generation""* (Acts 2:40). If they did this, they could be saved. For those that took Peter's advice on the Day of Pentecost, and all who subsequently put their trust in the crucified Messiah**, the tutelage of the law ceased** as they entered into full 'sonship': *"But now that faith has come,* **we are no longer under a tutor**. *For you are all sons of God through faith in Christ Jesus"* (Gal. 3:25–26 (NASB)).

Indeed, I would take it further. I would contend, that those Jews who still reject the Messianic claims of Jesus are also 'out of school' – they are no longer subject to the law of Moses – they are no longer under a tutor. Indeed, the tutor is no more – he has been dismissed and the instruments of law have been removed. The Jerusalem Temple is gone; the Aaronic High Priest has been replaced by the High Priest of the order of Melchizedek and the Aaronic priesthood is out of work. The Old Covenant has been superseded - the Messiah has come – and Hebrew people are required to respond to the gospel of grace in the same way as the Gentiles. Salvation by faith in the law, its rituals and sacrifices, is no longer available.

ALLEGORY 2: A LESSON FROM HISTORY

We cannot go back to keeping the law as a means of pleasing God – it is counter-productive. For those who contemplate keeping the festivals and such like, Paul would throw up his hands in despair: *"You observe days and months and seasons and years! I am afraid I may have laboured over you in vain"* (Gal. 4:10–11). The Galatians had been saved by the grace of God, and yet they were in danger of subjecting themselves to a bondage similar to that which held them prior to conversion, and from which they had been delivered. But how could this be? Had the Galatians actually renounced their Christian faith? Had they recanted? Did they no longer believe that Jesus was the promised Messiah? Certainly not! The temptation they faced, prompted by the Judaizing false teachers, was to doubt that Jesus Christ alone was sufficient for salvation. They were being told that it was necessary to add to their faith in Christ, circumcision and other outdated ceremonies of the Mosaic law. Yet to do this, Paul said, would be no different than succumbing to their former subservient obedience to worldly principles.[16]

To progress his argument, Paul references a most familiar family record, that of the father of the nation, first laying out some pertinent facts before interpreting them allegorically in rabbinical fashion. *"Tell me, you who desire to be under the law, do you not listen to the law? For it is written that Abraham had two sons, one by a slave woman and one by a free woman. But the son of the slave was born according to the flesh, while the son of the free woman was born through promise. Now this may be interpreted allegorically: these women are two covenants. One is from Mount Sinai, bearing children for slavery; she is Hagar. Now Hagar is Mount Sinai in Arabia; she corresponds to the present Jerusalem, for she is in slavery with her children. But the Jerusalem above is free, and she is our mother. For it is written, "Rejoice, O barren one who does not bear; break forth and cry aloud, you who are not in labour! For the children of the desolate one will be more than those of the one who has a husband." Now you, brothers, like Isaac, are children of promise. But just as at that time he who was born*

---

[16] Gal. 4:9; cf. Gal. 4:3

according to the flesh persecuted him who was born according to the Spirit, so also it is now. But what does the Scripture say? "Cast out the slave woman and her son, for the son of the slave woman shall not inherit with the son of the free woman" (Gal. 4:21-30).

Drawing from the history of the birth of Ishmael and Isaac, Paul offers several contrasts.

Law   is contrasted to promise

Hagar, the slave woman is contrasted to Sarah, the free woman

The child after the flesh is contrasted to the child of promise

The Old Covenant   is contrasted to the New Covenant

The earthly Jerusalem   is contrasted to the heavenly Jerusalem

He begins with that of first importance, that the son of Hagar, the slave woman, *"was born according to the flesh"*, while the son of Sarah *"was born through promise"*. Pursuing the analogy Paul states that Hagar *"corresponds to the present Jerusalem, for she is in slavery with her children"*. *"The present Jerusalem"* ... the city of Pharisees and Sadducees and Scribes - poor, proud, miserable Jerusalem, that was under slavery to the Romans and the still more bitter slavery of sin. The description of the Laodicean believers could have been applied to that last generation of Jerusalem law-keepers prior to the dissolution of the Mosaic Covenant - *"For you say, I am rich, I have prospered, and I need nothing, not realizing that you are wretched, pitiable, poor, blind, and naked. I counsel you to buy from me gold refined by fire, so that you may be rich, and white garments so that you may clothe yourself and the shame of your nakedness may not be seen, and salve to anoint your eyes, so that you may see. Those whom I love, I reprove and discipline, so be zealous and repent"* (Rev. 3:17–19). But Paul's words cannot be confined to the generation of Hebrews that were alive at the time of his writing – they surely imply that the Jewish nation is still acting as the child of the slave-mother, seeking to fulfil the law (as far as is possible) and are still in bondage. Not all, of course, for there are those of God's ancient people who have received their Messiah, entered the 'ekklesia' through grace and transfered their allegiance to Jerusalem above, for "*the Jerusalem above is free, and **she is our mother**"* (Gal. 4:26).

This historically important family history of the Patriarch provides Paul with that which was needed to formulate a warning for those toying with the possibility that the law had something to offer to enhance the Christian experience. He drives home the fact that the law is connected to the flesh, to bondage, to 'worldly' Jerusalem. To avoid misunderstanding Paul paraphrases Sarah's very blunt demand to make his point: "*Cast out the slave woman and her son, for the son of the slave woman shall not inherit with the son of the free woman*" (Gal. 4:30 cf. Gen. 21:10).

There is no ambiguity here! Cast out the bondwoman and her son, for the son of the bond-woman shall not be heir with the son of the free-woman! In respect to that which determines his continuing relationship to God, the child of God has nothing to do with the law! "*Let me ask you only this: Did you receive the Spirit by works of the law or by hearing with faith? Are you so foolish? Having begun by the Spirit, are you now being perfected by the flesh?*" (Gal. 3:2–3) Notice how easily Paul moves from "*law*" to "*flesh*". He aligns 'receiving the Spirit' with the 'hearing with faith', and equates the 'works of the law' to 'the flesh'. This is repeated later in the letter. "*But I say, walk by the Spirit, and you will not gratify the desires of the flesh. For the desires of the flesh are against the Spirit, and the desires of the Spirit are against the flesh, for these are opposed to each other, to keep you from doing the things you want to do. But if you are led by the Spirit, **you are not under the law**.*" (Gal. 5:16–18) In this passage he begins by setting the Spirit over against the flesh. For example, "*the desires of the flesh are against the Spirit*", but he concludes the paragraph by setting the Spirit over against the law, that is, "*But if you are led by the Spirit, **you are not under the law**.*" While law and flesh are not synonymous, they are, in Paul's mind, intimately related. The law may have its place in awakening an unbeliever to his sin but for those who name the name of Christ - they should be finished with it, "*we are not children of the slave but of the free woman*" (Gal. 4:31). In the clearest manner possible, Paul advocates that any attempt to insinuate law-keeping on those who have received the grace of God should be resisted. "*For freedom Christ has set us free; stand firm therefore, and do not submit* *again to a yoke of slavery"* (Gal. 5:1). Phillips' paraphrase presents it more vividly: *"do not let yourselves be caught again in the shackles of slavery"*.

Christian freedom has been called the inestimable blessing, the birthright of every believer. *"Christ has set us free"* – how those words should rejoice the heart.

> Free from the law, O happy condition,
>
> Jesus hath bled, and there is remission;
>
> Cursed by the law and bruised by the fall,
>
> grace hath redeemed us once for all.
>
> (Philip Paul Bliss)

On this foundation we should present ourselves to the world: *"stand firm therefore"*. When the freedom that justification has granted us begins to fade, or we start to lose sight of its incredible benefits, there is a temptation to lapse back into some kind of legalism. This temptation must be resisted at all costs: *"stand firm!"*

This freedom, of course, is not without its constraints: *"For you were called to freedom, brothers.* ***Only do not use your freedom as an opportunity for the flesh"*** (Gal. 5:13). It has obligations: *"through love serve one another"* (Gal. 5:13). Here then is revealed how the law, that has been put into heart and mind,[17] should be seen in action. Fulfilling the commands of the new covenant is what brings satisfaction to the heart of the Father, although they are more like beseechings rather than commands. "Love o*ne another"* (John 13:34; 15:12, 17; 1 Thes. 4:9; 1 Pet. 1:22; 1 John 3:11, 23; 4:7, 11; 2 John 5); *"husbands love your wives"* (Eph. 5:25; Col. 3:19); and young women should: *"love their husbands and children"* (Titus 2:4); each should *"love your neighbour as yourself"* (James 2:8). For *"the one who loves another*

---

[17] Heb. 8:10

has fulfilled the law" (Rom. 13:8), and there are no punishments published for failure although there is loss.

ALLEGORY 3: THE UNHAPPY MARRIAGE

In Romans Paul again draws on his Rabbinic training and offers a telling allegory. He speaks of those subject to the law as being married to it.[18] It is a marriage that is unhappy. The husband is a fine upstanding person – but he has standards that are impossible to meet. The wife, try as she may, cannot please him and he is unable to ease his demands. She is doomed to a life of misery because there is no possibility of divorce. Paul speaks of her being 'bound' to her husband. The marriage can only be dissolved on the death of either the husband or wife. But there is no possibility of the husband dying – this means that the wife will only be released from her contract by death. But, says the Apostle, for those that have embraced the salvation offered through Christ, this is exactly what happened. *"You ... have died to the law through the body of Christ, so that you may belong to another, to him who has been raised from the dead, in order that we may bear fruit for God"* (Rom. 7:4). This is an echo of his testimony presented in Galatians. *"For through the law I died to the law, so that I might live to God. I have been crucified with Christ. It is no longer I who live, but Christ who lives in me. And the life I now live in the flesh I live by faith in the Son of God, who loved me and gave himself for me."* (Gal. 2:19–20).

This new life that he is describing is contrasted to the old life of being married to the law. The old life was one of bondage, shackled to a husband who was unable to exercise any level of compassion or tolerance. But now – in union with Christ – what a glorious difference. Hear the Word of God - *"but now we are released from the law, having died to that which held us captive, so that we serve in the new way of the Spirit and not in the old way of the written code"* (Rom. 7:6). No longer 'bound' but 'released'; no longer

---

[18] Rom.7:1 ff.

'captive' but 'free'; no longer subject to the 'written code' but living 'in the new way of the Spirit'.

NOT ONE, NOT TWO, BUT THREE ALLEGORIES

For the Jewish people the combined weight of these three allegories is substantial – the first identifies the purpose of the law as that which was to prepare them to receive their Messiah. But His coming is now in the past. He came, He died, He rose and ascended – this means there is now no further need for the tutor (the law). The tutor has been dismissed and school is out! Members of the Hebrew race who have embraced the salvation their Messiah bought for them at unbelievable cost are no longer under the law – they are out of school! No need to return to keeping the feasts!

A consideration of the second allegory would pose the question for them. If you have been set free from slavery, why would you want to return? The T'nach tells us that the Exodus generation constantly looked back to Egypt. They thought the food of Egypt was better than the food YHWH provided. Many wanted to return, even after God had worked miracles to bring them out. Sin makes you foolish, like Esau who preferred a bowl of soup to his birthright. Occasionally we hear of the difficulty that some long-term prisoners experience when they are released. In prison they knew what to do – they had others to tell them when to rise and when to sleep, when to eat and when to work, etc. But once set free they are unable to adjust to life on the 'outside'. They commit a crime just to return to jail. They give up their freedom because living a life where 'the law' takes responsibility for their safety and their care seems more attractive. Is this the mind-set of some who, having been delivered from the law, now look back with longing to the days of Passover and Tabernacles and think that life 'under the law' was preferable to the unfettered life where every day is filled with choices and decisions?

Regarding the third allegory - who would want to return to an unhappy marriage? Indeed, since the marriage union with the law was dissolved with the aim of those that received their Messiah being betrothed to Him, returning to Torah observance is not only insulting to their future husband but tantamount to adultery (cf. Rom. 7:3-4).

And for those believers who are not of Jewish pedigree but are drawn to Torah-observance - why seek to place yourself under a tutor who has been dismissed? (allegory 1) Why put yourself in bondage when you are free? (allegory 2) Why seek a demanding and unyielding husband when you have fellowship with the Beloved Son of God? (allegory 3)

CHAPTER FIVE

LIGHT FROM THE CORINTHIAN CORRESPONDENCE

THE GLORY OF THE GOSPEL

The gospel that Paul preached was the eternal message of God, which is, 'saved by grace alone, through faith alone, in God alone'. In the age of grace, it is rephrased slightly - 'saved by grace alone, through faith alone, in Christ alone'. But like the Galatian churches, Corinth had been visited by those who preached 'another gospel' (cf. 11:4); a message that declared that salvation was only available through the door of the Mosaic covenant; that is, all had to convert to Judaism first; males had to be circumcised; and all had to be Torah obedient. The supporters of the back-to-Moses movement in the early Church followed Paul from place to place and tried to undermine his ministry. They contended that

(i)   Moses preceded Christ, and

(ii)   Christ was born under the law, and

(iii) Christ obeyed the law,

(iv)   It follows therefore, that Christ acknowledged the superiority of Moses.

(v)   Jesus was simply a part of the covenant that God mediated through Moses.

Paul had no difficulty in accepting that Jesus was a Torah observing Jew, but he contended the law was given to condition Israel to be the cradle into which God's Holy Son could be born. They would be the nation to be privileged to care for and nurture the One who would bring salvation to the ends of the earth; and if they responded with faith and obedience to His coming they would enjoy a multitude of national blessings. For Israel, the Torah culture instituted by God through Moses should have been the schoolmaster to lead them to Christ, as he indicated to the Galatian believers

(Gal. 3:24). It was purposed that His sacrificial death would be the final act of the Old Covenant which would then inaugurate the New Covenant. He would die at Passover, rise at the Feast of Firstfruits, to ascend forty days later and gift the Spirit of God to the waiting believers at the Feast of Weeks. The gift of the Holy Spirit would be the mechanism which would scribe the mind and knowledge of God on the hearts of believers, in fulfilment of the New Covenant *"I will put my law within them, and I will write it on their hearts. And I will be their God, and they shall be my people. And no longer shall each one teach his neighbour and each his brother, saying, 'Know the* LORD,*' for they shall all know me, from the least of them to the greatest, declares the* LORD. *For I will forgive their iniquity, and I will remember their sin no more""* (Jer. 31:33–34).

Since Paul's opponents contended that the Mosaic covenant was still current, in the Corinthian letters he countered their argument by drawing contrasts between the Mosaic Covenant and the New Covenant. He first said that the New is superior to the Old. The Old had a glory which has faded. Using the motif of Exodus 34.29-34 he referred to the reflected glory that Moses enjoyed: *"When Moses came down from Mount Sinai, with the two tablets of the testimony in his hand as he came down from the mountain, Moses did not know that the skin of his face shone because he had been talking with God. Aaron and all the people of Israel saw Moses, and behold, the skin of his face shone, and they were afraid to come near him. But Moses called to them, and Aaron and all the leaders of the congregation returned to him, and Moses talked with them. Afterward all the people of Israel came near, and he commanded them all that the* LORD *had spoken with him in Mount Sinai. And when Moses had finished speaking with them, he put a veil over his face. Whenever Moses went in before the* LORD *to speak with him, he would remove the veil, until he came out. And when he came out and told the people of Israel what he was commanded"* (Exod. 34:29–34). The reflected glory that Moses enjoyed faded, and the Old covenant has faded likewise. However, the New has a glory which will never fade. On the Damascus Road Paul saw the glory of the risen Christ and that glory was, and is, inherent and eternal. And not only is the New superior, it is the only means of reconciliation available. The Old was temporary and is now abolished: *"what was being brought to an end"* (2 Cor. 3:11). The New is current and eternal: *"what is permanent"* (2 Cor. 3:11).

The Old mediated condemnation and death, and is accordingly called both *"the ministry of death"* (2 Cor. 3:7) and *"the ministry of condemnation"* (2 Cor. 3:9). The New mediates righteousness and peace and is properly titled *"the ministry of righteousness"* (2 Cor. 3:9).

The transition from the Old to the New took place with the coming of Israel's Messiah, the Saviour of the world. The timetable provided by the Mosaic economy was followed exactly. Jesus died at Passover giving completion and meaning to all the sacrifices offered in Tabernacle and Temple. His death provided a sacrifice of such worth that it subdued the wrath of God (propitiation); satisfied the righteousness of God (expiation); recompensed God for the loss He had suffered (compensation); and provided the two cleansing agents under the Mosaic economy that purify - blood and water (purification).

This mighty act, the sacrificial death of Christ, completely changed the method of approach to God. The method of mediation under the old dispensation was through the Aaronic priesthood that had been set up by Moses and operated on the basis of the charter provided at Sinai. But that changed when Jesus came. Mediation under the New Covenant is set out clearly: *"For there is one God, and there is one mediator between God and men, the man Christ Jesus, who gave himself as a ransom for all"* (1 Tim. 2:5–6). That Jesus is the mediator is confirmed in 5:18 ff: *"All this is from God, who through Christ reconciled us to himself and gave us the ministry of reconciliation"* (2 Cor. 5:18), which is why Paul constantly declares *"For what we proclaim is not ourselves, but Jesus Christ as Lord, with ourselves as your servants for Jesus' sake"* (2 Cor. 4:5). The essence of this mediatorial ministry is what is at the heart of the well-known verse from chapter 1. *"For all the promises of God find their Yes in him. That is why it is through him that we utter our Amen to God for his glory"* (2 Cor. 1:20).

He is the 'Yes' to Gen.3.15 (the seed of the woman to bruise the Serpent's head).

He is the 'Yes' to the Abrahamic Covenant that through a descendent of Abraham "*all the families of the earth shall be blessed*" (Gen.12:3).

He is the 'Yes' to the Davidic Covenant which promised a son of David to reign on David's throne (2 Sam. 7:11ff).

He is the 'Yes' to the New Covenant which promised: "*I will put my law within them, and I will write it on their hearts. And I will be their God, and they shall be my people*" (Jer. 31:33).

Chapter 5 also contrasts the Old and New and points to the substitutionary death of Christ as being the foundation for our new life in Him. "*Therefore, if anyone is in Christ, he is a new creation. The old has passed away; behold, the new has come. All this is from God, who through Christ reconciled us to himself and gave us the ministry of reconciliation; that is, in Christ God was reconciling the world to himself, not counting their trespasses against them, and entrusting to us the message of reconciliation. Therefore, we are ambassadors for Christ, God making his appeal through us. We implore you on behalf of Christ, be reconciled to God. For our sake he made him to be sin who knew no sin, so that in him we might become the righteousness of God. Working together with him, then, we appeal to you not to receive the grace of God in vain*" (2 Cor. 5:17–6:1). There is no reference to the Mosaic covenant or the law in this summary. It is true that you cannot draw firm conclusions from the silence of Scripture but if obedience to the law played any essential part in their experience of salvation surely it should be included here.

God does not simply make a book-keeping alteration by dropping the charges against us. God gives himself to us in friendship. Because of our extreme hostility toward Him, this investment is accomplished at unspeakable cost. "*For our sake he made him to be sin who knew no sin, so that in him we might become the righteousness of God*" (2 Cor. 5:21). It cannot be that the death of Christ is in any way insufficient. It does not need any Torah obedience to complete it.

CHAPTER SIX

LIGHT FROM THE LETTER TO THE EPHESIANS

THE LAW A WALL OF SEPARATION

The letter to the Ephesians touches on our subject from 2:11 forward where Paul begins to describe how Jew and Gentile had been, prior to the ascension of the Messiah, two separate people groups as far as the purposes of God were concerned. The Jews, under the Old Covenant, were a separated people with a God-given regime that governed their social, religious and national behaviour. Gentiles (unless they decided to convert) were kept at a distance. Israel's Temple practices reflected this separation. Gentiles were allowed to enter the Temple Mount but only as observers. The main Temple courts, those of Israel, of Prayer, of the Israelites, of the Priests, were all out of bounds to the 'uncircumcised'. This separation was given a physical dimension by a three cubit (4 ft. 6 ins.) wall of partition in which there were some 13 gates. At each gate there was a notice which said, 'No stranger is to enter within the balustrade around the Temple and its enclosure. Whoever is caught will be responsible for his own death, which will ensue'.[19] This notice was supported by the presence of a Temple guard at each gate. Thus was evidenced the fact that the law of Moses was an instrument that separated Jew and Gentile. Paul refers to this separation in the most animated of language: "*remember that you were at that time ... alienated from the commonwealth of Israel and strangers to the covenants of promise, having no hope and without God in the world*" (Eph. 2:12).

But the death of the Messiah changed all that: "*But now in Christ Jesus you who once were far off have been brought near by the blood of Christ.*" (Eph. 2:13) Hallelujah! How did He do this? He "*has broken down in his flesh the dividing wall of hostility*" (Eph. 2:14). "*The dividing wall of hostility*" –

---

[19] The Splendour of the Temple by Alec Garrard (Moat Farm Publications) (1997) p.46

what a description, how apt an allusion to the forbidding wall in the Temple which threatened death to any Gentile that breached it. But it has been demolished, taken out of the way. But how? How did the Messiah, who has ultimate authority in these matters, accomplish this mighty act of grace? Not by removing the actual wall of separation – but rather by removing what it represented. He abolished *"the law of commandments expressed in ordinances, that he might create in himself one new man in place of the two, so making peace"* (Eph. 2:15). There is now no need for the 'law', no need for a 'wall of separation' because Jew and Gentile are received on the same basis. The result has been a blessing to both Jew and Gentile from that time to this. *"And he came and preached peace to you who were far off* (the Gentiles) *and peace to those who were near* (the Jews). *For through him we both have access in one Spirit to the Father"* (Eph. 2:17–18). *"We both"* in this verse is a reference to Jewish and Gentile believers. The 'one new man' is the Church. Identified in Scripture are now three people groups – unbelieving Jews (referred to as Israel in the New Testament); unbelieving Gentiles; and the Church (made up of believing Jews and believing Gentiles). The believing Gentiles are now *"no longer strangers and aliens, but ... fellow citizens with the saints and members of the household of God"* (Eph. 2:19).

This people group, the Church, is described as a structure, joined together, growing into a holy temple in the Lord, built together into a dwelling place for God by the Spirit.[20] No difference between Jew and Gentile believer. Both have been saved by grace alone, through faith alone, in Christ alone. The wall of separation, the law, has been removed and that which was implemented after the exodus to keep Israel separate from the nations has been abolished. Now *"there is neither Jew nor Greek, there is neither slave nor free, there is no male and female, for* (we) *are all one in Christ Jesus"* (Gal. 3:28). Those of Jewish descent should be rejoicing because *"the law of commandments expressed in ordinances"* has been abolished and

---

[20] Eph. 2:21-22

Gentiles should be equally happy for they have access to the blessing of the Abrahamic covenant without having to submit to the Mosaic covenant.[21]

This mighty act, the creation of the Church, which is now a building inhabited by the Spirit of God and will be the bride of Christ, was accomplished by his sacrifice by which He rid the world of those laws, judgements and ordinances that could only condemn. To the Colossians he declared that the Messiah, in dying by crucifixion, dealt a fatal blow to the law, "*by cancelling the record of debt that stood against us with its legal demands. This he set aside, nailing it to the cross*" (Col. 2:14).

PAUL, A STEWARD OF GOD'S GRACE

The truth, that Jew and Gentile should now fellowship in the Lord Jesus with no hindrances, leads Paul to express to these Ephesian believers whom he loves, further testimony of his place in the promulgation of this Jewish/Gentile harmony in Christ. Jesus, the head of the Church,[22] personally revealed to Paul this truth of the creation of this new entity that had been unknown to those of the former dispensation of law. Paul describes it: "*This mystery ... that the Gentiles are fellow heirs, members of the same body, and partakers of the promise in Christ Jesus through the gospel*" (Eph. 3:6). That which was previously unknown, and is now revealed, that Jew and Gentile (both saved in the same way, that is by grace) should constitute the body of Christ is of such sophistication and magnitude that it reveals the *"manifold wisdom of God"*. "*Oh, the depth of the riches and wisdom and knowledge of God! How unsearchable are his judgments and how inscrutable his ways!*" (Rom. 11:33) Paul magnifies his office: "*Of this gospel I was made a minister according to the gift of God's grace, which was given me by the working of his power. To me, though I am the very least of all the saints, this grace was given, to preach to the Gentiles the unsearchable riches of Christ, and to bring to light for everyone what is the*

---

[21] See my book "The Messiah and the Covenants of Israel" for a fuller treatment (Published by Gospel Folio Press, Port Colborne (2009))

[22] Eph. 1:22; 4:15; 5:23

plan of the mystery hidden for ages in God who created all things, so that through the church the manifold wisdom of God might now be made known to the rulers and authorities in the heavenly places. This was according to the eternal purpose that he has realized in Christ Jesus our Lord" (Eph. 3:7– 11).

So the Apostle was commissioned to bear particular responsibilities as a servant of Christ,[23] an ambassador for Christ,[24] and particularly a steward[25] of Christ's *"unsearchable riches"*. As steward of *"God's grace"* he had responsibility to enjoy God's grace; to glory in God's grace; to preach God's grace; to defend the truth of God's grace. Anyone that suggested there was anything that improved or supplanted God's grace found in Paul a fierce and resolute opponent. What was true then is still true now – grace reigns supreme (not law).[26]

---

[23] Rom. 1:1; Gal. 1:10, etc.
[24] Eph. 6:20
[25] Eph. 3:2
[26] Rom. 5:21

CHAPTER SEVEN

LIGHT FROM THE BOOK OF HEBREWS

THE MESSIAH – THE SUPERIOR MEDIATOR

The Hebrew epistle is the second of the great theological letters of the New Testament. It was written to deal with a particular problem. How should Messianic Jews relate to the law of Moses with its regulations regarding sacrifices, offerings, festivals and priestly intercession? It seeks to answer the question; does the Mosaic Covenant still have a part to play in the period after the sacrifice of Messiah on Golgotha? This addresses the very question under review.

Early in the letter the writer lays out the greatness of Moses and Aaron and does not minimize the value of the sacerdotal culture of Israel that these two mighty men of God initiated - a culture that had held Israel together for millennia. However, he recognized that it was instituted for a particular purpose and once that purpose was accomplished the need for it ceased. The transition from the Old Covenant, (spoken by angels, mediated by Moses and maintained by the Aaronic priesthood), to the New Covenant, (initiated, maintained and mediated by Messiah), took place at the first Feast of Weeks after the death of the Christ. Once the age of the New Covenant began, the need for the Mosaic code, with its call for sin, trespass and sweet savour offerings, expired. Once the Messiah had died as the Lamb of God the necessity for daily and annual sacrifices of lambs from the Temple flocks ceased. Once the Saviour had made atonement for sin, the Day of Atonement rituals were no longer needed. But the change demanded by the new regime was so radical, and the habit of looking toward Jerusalem, with its Temple, High Priest and Festivals, was so entrenched, that even for those who had accepted the person and office of the Messiah there was an uncertainty. The rituals that they had followed for the whole of their adult life exercised a magnetic attraction – an attraction which increased greatly during times when Messianic Jews were persecuted for their loyalty to Christ. So the writer offers guidance and encouragement and sometimes sounds a warning to his readers. He calls on them to fully commit to the New Covenant for two main reasons – firstly, because of its superiority to the Old Covenant – and secondly, it is the only pathway to obtain forgiveness of sins and a relationship with God.

MEDIATION TO, FOR, AND BY, ISRAEL

Perhaps the main purpose of the call of Israel was, that she should provide a means of mediation between the God of heaven and fallen humanity. Mediation was to be their study and their life. They had themselves initially been the recipients of mediation through angels and Moses; but in the day to day activity of the nation Aaron and his descendants occupied the office of mediators, interceding for the people and bringing their sacrifices and offerings. The Tabernacle (later the Temple), the place of mediation, was the centre of the nation. The transfer of the baton of mediation took place in the following fashion:

First, the message was committed to angels to deliver as intimated by Heb. 2:2-3: *"For since **the message declared by angels** proved to be reliable, and every transgression or disobedience received a just retribution, how shall we escape if we neglect such a great salvation?"*

These angelic messengers committed it to Moses, who had been chosen, called and gifted to bear such a responsibility.[27]

Moses then committed the code, which specified the principles of life and conduct by which Israel was to live, to the tribe of Levi, who had been taken by the Lord in lieu of the firstborn of Israel and commissioned to serve the Sanctuary where the sacerdotal function was to operate.

The tribe of Levi was divided into four – the primary group were those of the family of Aaron who would constitute the priesthood and function

---

[27] Moses had been chosen as the mediator from Israel's side, to the degree that there are times when it is spoken of as 'Moses' law' (Heb. 10:28).

as the day to day mediators between Israel and God. They would be aided by the families of Kohath, Gershon and Merari whose main responsibility during the period of Tabernacle worship would be as erectors and transporters of the wood, metal and fabric of the Tabernacle. During the Temple period they provided support personnel such as the Temple guard. In this way, the tribe of Levi was corporately responsible for the functioning of the Mosaic code. However, the Sanctuary, the Priesthood, the Offerings, the Festivals, were only:

> *"the **copy and shadow** of the heavenly things"* (Heb. 8:5):

> *"**a shadow of the good things to come** instead of the true form of these realities"* (Heb. 10:1):

> *"**copies** of the true things"* (Heb. 9:24) and

> *"**copies** of the heavenly things"* (Heb. 9:23).

In contrast, the death of the Messiah was the reality set over against the shadow, and therefore superior to anything Israel could experience under the law. Nevertheless, the national structure imposed on Israel by God was enough to demonstrate how the execution of Jesus could be the sin offering to cap all sin offerings – a sin offering that would fully satisfy the claims of the God of heaven who is holy, righteous, loving, merciful, forgiving and long-suffering.

What is asserted here is a declaration that the mediation of Christ transcends all previous mediation. He is the pre-eminent mediator and indeed in the current dispensation, because of His sacrifice, the only mediator: *"For there is one God, and there is one mediator between God and men, the man Christ Jesus, who gave himself as a ransom for all"* (1 Tim. 2:5–6).

If He is the only mediator the need for the former instruments of mediation (the priesthood, the temple, the festivals, the sacrifices) has expired.

WHY IS CHRIST'S MEDIATION SUPERIOR?

1. It is superior because of who He is - He is God's Son and the Clearest Message to Humankind: *"long ago, at many times and in many ways, God spoke to our fathers by the prophets, but in these last days he has spoken to us by **his Son**"* (Heb. 1:1–2).

    Not only bringing the word from God but coming as the Word of God. If we accept the revelation of *"His Son"*, we receive and know the mind and will of God. As Son He has been: *"appointed the heir of all things"* (Heb. 1:2).

    As Son of Abraham He is heir to the land;

    as Son of David He is heir to the throne;

    as Son of Man He is heir to the world; and

    as Son of God He is heir to all things.

2. He is the executive arm of the Godhead: *"through whom also he created the world"* (Heb.1:2), which emphasizes the beginning of history. He is the alpha of it, the beginning of it.

3. He is the perfect manifestation of God: *"the express imprint of his nature"* (Heb. 1:3). Everything that is true of God the Father is true of God the Son. All the attributes of the Father are in the Son - He is God *"manifest in the flesh"* (1 Tim. 3:16 KJV).

4. He is the sustainer and governor of the Universe: *"he upholds the universe by the word of his power"* (Heb. 1:3). Not only created through Him but also maintained by Him. *"Upholds"* or *"sustains"* (as per the NRSV) carries the meaning 'bears along' and gives the sense that He is moving everything along to a pre-determined goal.

5. He has the highest place that heaven affords: *"He … sat down at the right hand of the Majesty on high"* (Heb. 1:3). To sit at the right hand means equality. The Son sat at the right hand of the Father - it means

He has equal majesty - He is sovereign. But He sits as a King/Priest which means He has finished His work.

CHRIST'S SUPERIORITY IS DEMONSTRATED BY COMPARISONS

The importance and gravity of any message from heaven is often revealed in the dignity, importance and authority of the messenger. The author of the letter is going to draw on his knowledge of previous mediators sent by heaven with instructions from the throne, and compare and contrast them with God's greatest and ultimately sole mediator, Christ.

1. BETTER THAN PROPHETS

The first comparison, at the very beginning of the letter, is that the revelation brought by the Lord Jesus is far superior to anything vouchsafed to the prophets, even those considered great in Jewish history, such as David and Isaiah. They only had snippets of light whereas "the Son" has the whole counsel of God: "*Long ago, at many times and in many ways, God spoke to our fathers by the prophets, but in these last days he has spoken to us by his Son*" (Heb. 1:1–2).

Prior to His coming God had spoken to many individuals using different means of communication. They heard, they saw, they felt, yet each only saw a part. All was not revealed to any single person. Abraham understood He would be of his posterity; to Jacob was revealed the tribe to which He would belong (Judah); David had an assurance that He would be of his family; Micah received information regarding the place of His birth; and Daniel was given the time He would come. Isaiah and Malachi knew of the ministry of His forerunner, and so on… Each only knew in part; but when that which was perfect came in Messiah, that which was in part was done away.[28] The comparison with the prophets is soon followed by a comparison with the

---

[28] Cf. 1 Cor. 13:12

chief contributors to the transmission of the law by which Israel was to live, angels and Moses.

2. BETTER THAN ANGELS

He is *"superior to angels"* (Heb. 1:4). This comparison demands that we define the greatness and glory of angelic beings as revealed in Scripture. Angels are mentioned over 200 times in the Old Testament with some 186 references in the New. Only very occasionally used as a description of men; it almost always refers to a heavenly messenger that God has charged with some commission. Sometimes, of course, it refers to the Lord of angels rather than the created beings.

They are spirit beings (Heb. 1:14) and have been created (Ps. 148.2-5; Job 38.6,7). They are innumerable (Heb. 12:22), of a higher order than man (Heb. 2:7) with greater wisdom (2 Sam. 14:20) and greater power (Matt. 28.2; Acts 5.19; 2 Pet. 2.11). There are some that hold office as governmental rulers (Eph. 6:12) and some honoured to hold high office like Michael and Gabriel who are archangels with special responsibilities. Michael, called 'great prince' in Daniel 12.1 is commissioned to defend Israel (Rev. 12.7-9) whereas Gabriel appears to be the one to whom is committed those special messages for humanity regarding the purposes of God (Dan. 9; Matt. 1; Luke 1, etc.). In addition, there is Lucifer, the 'shining one' who is spoken of as being the wisest and most beautiful and who had authority over cherubim and seraphim (cf. Isa. 14 and Ezek. 28).

Angels are particular servants of the Godhead. To cherubim is committed the defence of the holiness of God (not that God needs defending but He has elected that they should be so engaged). Seraphim surround the throne and also attend to His holiness.

Since angels are commissioned to serve the Godhead it is both significant and appropriate that they should have ministered to the Messiah. They announced His birth (Luke 2:9 ff.); protected His infancy (Matt. 2:13); strengthened Him after the temptation (Matt. 4:11); encouraged Him in Gethsemane (Luke 22:43); announced His resurrection (Matt. 28:5-7); and attended His ascension (Acts 1:10). They will also accompany Him at His second coming (Matt. 25:31).

But the 'Son' is better, greater, of higher dignity and worthy of more honour than any and all of the angels. The writer uses six quotations from the T'nach to support his statement, harmonizing with his opening paragraph in praise of the 'Son'.

1. *"For to which of the angels did God ever say, "You are my Son, today I have begotten you"?* (cf. Ps.2:7)

2. *"and again: "I will be to him a father, and he shall be to me a son"?"* (Heb. 1:5 cf. 2 Sam.7:14) The greatness and glory of angels is unquestionable, but they are servants to deity whereas Jesus is the Son of the Father.

3. *"And again, when he brings the firstborn into the world, he says, "Let all God's angels worship him""* (Heb. 1:6; based on Ps. 97:7). In this quote we are allowed to know of a command from the throne for angels to do homage to the infant Christ-child.

4. *"But of the Son he says, "Your throne, O God, is forever and ever, the sceptre of uprightness is the sceptre of your kingdom. You have loved righteousness and hated wickedness; therefore God, your God, has anointed you with the oil of gladness beyond your companions""* (Heb. 1:8,9; cf. Ps.45:6,7). Angels receive instructions from the Godhead, whereas the Son is a member of that Godhead holding the emblems of authority over all created beings and ruling in righteousness.

5. This is supported by a further quote, this time from Psalm 102 (vv.25-27): *"You, Lord, laid the foundation of the earth in the beginning, and the heavens are the work of your hands; they will perish, but you remain; they will all wear out like a garment, like a robe you will roll them up, like a garment they will be changed. But you are the same, and your years will have no end"* (Heb. 1:10–12).

6.   And then again (from Ps. 110.1) *"But to which of the angels has He ever said: 'Sit at My right hand, Till I make Your enemies Your footstool'?"* (Hebrews 1:13)

The writer has been especially wise in his selection of Messianic verses with which his readers would have been familiar. He has used them to establish the deity of Messiah and in their original settings has taken the readers on a journey from the resurrection and ascension of the Son of God through this present age to His coming reign on earth and beyond.

Building on the high regard that the Jewish people had for angels the writer offers a warning. *"Therefore we must pay much closer attention to what we have heard, lest we drift away from it. For since the message declared by angels proved to be reliable, and every transgression or disobedience received a just retribution, how shall we escape if we neglect such a great salvation? It was declared at first by the Lord, and it was attested to us by those who heard, while God also bore witness by signs and wonders and various miracles and by gifts of the Holy Spirit distributed according to his will"* (Heb. 2:1–4).

This is designed to direct his readers to the vital nature of the sacrifice of the Messiah by declaring the importance of the message brought by *'the LORD'* and confirmed by those He commissioned. If the message brought by angels had severe consequences for those who disregarded – how much more severe would the consequences be for those who neglected the offer of salvation brought by the Son of God. So here is placed a warning which arises out of the context of angels. If the covenant mediated by angels required such diligence and attention, how much more the covenant mediated by Christ who is Lord of the angels and who holds the highest office and is destined for ultimate triumph. When the author of the Hebrew letter declares: *"Therefore we must pay much closer attention to what we have heard, lest we drift away from it.* (Heb. 2.1), he is warning his readers about neglect: *"how shall we escape if we neglect such a great salvation"* (Heb. 2:3). This neglect carries the highest risk since it relates to our ultimate destiny.

When he returns to his main theme he indicates that even though Michael and the archangels are powerful they will not be in charge of the world to come. *"For it was not to angels that God subjected the world to come, of which we are speaking. It has been testified somewhere, "What is man, that you are mindful of him, or the son of man, that you care for him? You made him for a little while lower than the angels; you have crowned him with glory and honour, putting everything in subjection under his feet. Now in putting everything in subjection to him, he left nothing outside his control. At present, we do not yet see everything in subjection to him. But we see him who for a little while was made lower than the angels, namely Jesus, crowned with glory and honour because of the suffering of death, so that by the grace of God he might taste death for everyone"* (Heb. 2:5–9). He uses the name 'Jesus' reminding the readers that He became man to taste death for every man, so they should not be ashamed to be associated with Him.

The Hebrew epistle is addressed to believers who were suffering. Suffering for Jews was nothing new. But these were suffering by the hand of Jews as well as others. And there was shame associated with this suffering. Jesus was crucified. He had been abused, spat upon, hung naked on a tree and subjected to the Biblical curse. So these readers had to be reminded that He is the King of Glory, not simply the man of sorrows. On the other hand, they will be exhorted, before the end of the letter, to identify with the man of sorrows. *"So Jesus also suffered outside the gate in order to sanctify the people through his own blood. Therefore let us go to him outside the camp and bear the reproach he endured"* (13:12–13).

They were also reminded that He could have escaped. Peter was advised when he tried to defend the Saviour with a sword, *"Do you think that I cannot appeal to my Father, and he will at once send me more than twelve legions of angels?"* (Matt. 26:53) Twelve legions equate to something like 50,000 angels. Consider this statement in the light of the fact that only one angel was needed to defeat the army of Sennacherib (2 Chron.32:21).

To take upon Himself the nature of angels would have been consistent with the T'nach. It is understood that references to the 'Angel of the Lord' in the Old Testament often refer to the pre-incarnate Christ. Examples include the episode when Jacob wrestled by the brook Jabbok (Gen. 32:24 cf. 48:16); and Joshua planned the overthrow of Jericho (Josh. 5:13 ff). Then there was Gideon in Judges chapter 6 and Manoah in Judges chapter 13. Manoah's experience is particularly interesting for when he was visited by the Angel of the Lord he asked his celestial visitor *"What is your name, so that, when your words come true, we may honour you?"* He received the reply, *"Why do you ask my name, seeing it is wonderful?"* (Judges 13:17–18). 'Wonderful' as a name is used again in Isaiah, *"And his name shall be called Wonderful, Counsellor, The mighty God, The everlasting Father, The Prince of Peace"* (Isaiah 9:6, KJV). Manoah said to his wife, *"We shall surely die, for we have seen God"* (Judges 13:22).

As Lord of the Angels, and on times the Angel of the Lord, He could have taken on Himself the nature of angels - but He did not. Because He was not intending to aid angels but rather the seed of Abraham (and through them - humanity). To aid the Jewish nation it was necessary to be a kinsman, and ultimately a kinsman redeemer: ***"Therefore he had to be made like his brothers in every respect,*** *so that he might become a merciful and faithful high priest in the service of God, to make propitiation for the sins of the people"* (Heb. 2:17).

And this was in harmony with God's purpose and character. *"For it was fitting that he, for whom and by whom all things exist, in bringing many sons to glory, should make the founder of their salvation perfect through suffering. For he who sanctifies and those who are sanctified all have one source. That is why he is not ashamed to call them brothers"* (Heb. 2:10–11).

3. BETTER THAN MOSES

Chapter three of the epistle reminds the reader that the Messiah, *"the Apostle and High Priest of our confession"* (Heb. 3:1) is still the central figure under consideration. Having favourably compared His ministry of mediation to that of angels he continues by making a comparison with the mighty prophet Moses. Consider how great this man Moses was. He was the hero of the Jewish people. His many ministries to the nation included being their:

Deliverer (he was instrumental in their escape from servitude in Egypt).

Mediator (he received and then imparted to the nation those instructions regarding the priestly culture that provided the basis for the nation to be God's special treasure).

Guide/Shepherd (he had a key role in leading them from Egypt to Canaan).

Prophet (he was an important link in the chain of revelation – he received the oracles of God and gave them an ethical code by which to live. Furthermore, he indicated that he would be the template by which they could identify the coming Messiah).

Historian (he left a permanent record, not only of the early history of the nation, but also of key events in the history of the world prior to their enslavement in Egypt).

Legislator (he established and recorded the law by which the nation should live).

Orator (his speeches were recorded to provide a continual challenge to every member of the Hebrew people to love, honour and obey the God of heaven).

The writer of the Hebrew letter, in seeking to magnify the person and ministry of the Messiah, does not seek to minimize the contribution that Moses made to the establishment and survival of Israel and declares He "*was faithful*" (Heb. 3:2). While both Jesus and Moses were faithful in their allotted ministries Jesus is considered worthy of more honour and more glory than Moses because of a major difference in duty and status. Using a familiar designation *"house"*, the author of the letter draws a contrast: *"Now Moses was faithful in all God's house as a servant, to testify to the things that were to be spoken later, but Christ is faithful over God's house as a son."* (Heb. 3:5–6)

Although there are several groupings that could be designated 'house' that would fit the ministry of Moses, in all, Moses was a servant, albeit a faithful servant, whereas Christ established it, that is, conceived it and built it. *"For Jesus has been counted worthy of more glory than Moses—as much more glory as the builder of a house has more honour than the house itself"* (Heb. 3:3–4). Here then is another declaration of the divine status of Christ, the builder of the house: *(For every house is built by someone, but the builder of all things is God.)"* (Heb. 3:4).

In these texts (Heb. 3:3-6) the comparison between Moses, the servant in the house, and Jesus, the Son over the house, recognises the superiority of Christ. In this way the writer establishes that Moses, great as he was, is eclipsed by the greatness of God's Messiah. Moses, if he were available for advice, would echo the Baptist – *"he who is coming after me is mightier than I"* (Matt. 3:11) ... *"He must increase, but I must decrease"* (John 3:30). John, described as the greatest prophet of the Old Dispensation, had no claim on the allegiance of his disciples. He was required to point them to the Messiah and recommend allegiance to Him. **Moses' disciples should follow the example of John's disciples and likewise fully commit to the Messiah.**

The author of the letter has emphasized that the greatness of the Lord Jesus exceeds that of prophets, angels and Moses. **These comparisons were the necessary preliminaries to a consideration of the superiority of His High Priesthood and sacrifice, which was designed to encourage those that read the letter to commit fully to the New Covenant and not feel they have either been disobedient to the commandments of the T'nach or disloyal to the culture of the fathers.**

This section, demonstrating as it does the superiority of the mediation of Christ over that of Moses, will ultimately lead us to see the superiority of grace over law. The law came by Moses, but grace came by Jesus Christ – and to the same degree that Moses has been eclipsed by the Son of God, law has been eclipsed by grace.

CHAPTER EIGHT

LIGHT FROM THE BOOK OF HEBREWS

THE MESSIAH – THE SUPERIOR HIGH PRIEST

The Priestly protocol in which the Hebrew nation had been educated was familiar to those to whom the Hebrew letter was addressed. Consequently, the writer had the confidence to demonstrate how Christ was the reality set over against the Old Covenant shadow; the Anti-type set over against the type. Having demonstrated that the Messiah was superior to both angels and Moses as a mediator, he turns his attention to the priestly culture of Israel and sets himself the task of demonstrating how the person and work of the Lord Jesus was superior in this category also. He considers four areas – the priesthood; the sanctuary in which the priest served; the sacrifice which the priest offered; and the covenant under which the priest operated.

THE PRIESTHOOD OF CHRIST

This priestly theme is the principle subject of the Hebrew letter from 4:14 to 10:3. In these chapters Jesus is presented as the High Priest who crowned the sacerdotal revelation. He provided the mechanism by which humanity can be reconciled to God, as well as representing those who had received His saving ministry in the presence of the Father.

The inspired writer, having declared that Jesus is our High Priest,[29] calls on a text in Psalms to point to a mysterious king/priest who met with Abraham[30]. With these Scriptures he establishes that there is another order of High Priest, a higher order, that of Melchizedek, and that the High Priestly call of the eternal Son of God could only have been to that order.

---

[29] Heb. 4:14
[30] Gen. 14:18 ff

Nevertheless, the heavenly-provided pattern that governed the Aaronic priesthood would also be the pattern for the ministry of His Melchizedekian priesthood, since the Aaronic priesthood was the shadow of a reality into which the ministry of the Messiah as High Priest would fit.

BETTER THAN AARON

Consider how great this man Aaron was. Chosen, called and gifted as the first High Priest of Israel, he stood in the presence of God bearing the names of the twelve tribes over his heart and on his shoulders. His intercession was key to the health and preservation of the nation. His ministry set the pattern for all subsequent High Priests. The priesthood that was commissioned to protect and prosper the Hebrew people bears his name. Nevertheless, Christ is greater than Aaron and His priesthood better than the Aaronic as we shall see.

Consider how long and how thorough the education of the nation had been. They were brought to understand the need for suitable mediators between them and their God. These mediators were drawn from the tribe of Levi and the family of Aaron; men who were called and trained for their ministry. Daily, during the many hundreds of years when the Tabernacle/Temple was functioning, Israelites were able to observe the priests obeying the law, reciting their prayers, offering sacrifices and interceding for the nation. But while the Aaronic priesthood served a valuable purpose in Israel's history it was inevitably leading them to the time when it would be needed no more; a time when God would call a High Priest of a higher order than that of Aaron, to present a *"once for all"* sacrifice,[31] which would bring the sacerdotal system of reconciliation to its peak and quench the need for further sacrifices. The author of Hebrews is clear in his understanding – the death of Christ was a multi-layered sacrifice that met all the criteria.

He was the High Priest of a God-ordained order (that of Melchizedek).

---

[31] Rom. 6:10; Heb. 7:27; 9:12; 9:26; 10:10; Jude 3

His life was a sacrifice that was not only for sin, but also presented as a sweet savour to God.

It was sacrificed in the right year (according to Daniel's prophecy (Dan. 9); on the right day (the Day of the Passover); at the right time (the time of the evening sacrifice); in the right place ('outside the camp'), in the right way (by being lifted up).

As High Priest He functions in the heavenly sanctuary (albeit that which was typified by the Temple which stood in the shadow of Golgotha).

The blood of His sacrifice inaugurated and sanctified the 'New Covenant' which replaced the Mosaic Covenant which had fulfilled its purpose.

In summary, His was a superior sacrifice, offered in a superior sanctuary, presented by a superior High Priest establishing a superior covenant. This High Priestly office was taken up and occupied to intercede for those who recognize Him as such, that is, those who take Him as **their** High Priest. It is an office for which He is uniquely qualified; established on the pattern of the Aaronic High Priest but discharged as a Melchizedekian High Priest with higher qualifications and generating greater blessing. So let us "... *consider Jesus, the ... high priest of our confession*" (Heb. 3:1).

HIS QUALIFICATIONS FOR OFFICE: 1. THE INCARNATION

Here is revealed the necessity for the incarnation. A priest must be a true representative of those for whom he intercedes, more so the High Priest. This is observed by the writer to the Hebrews: "*For every high priest chosen from among men is appointed to act on behalf of men in relation to God, to offer gifts and sacrifices for sins*" (Heb. 5:1). Jesus was truly human, and necessarily so if He were to intercede for humanity before the throne of God: "*Therefore he had to be made like his brothers in every respect, so that he might become a merciful and faithful high priest in the service of God, to make propitiation for the sins of the people*" (Heb. 2:17).

This necessity is fleshed out in other verses. Because He was *"born of woman, born under the law"* (Gal. 4:4), He experienced first-hand those pressures that are the regular lot of humankind. *"For because he himself has suffered when tempted, he is able to help those who are being tempted"* (Heb. 2:18), and *"He can deal gently with the ignorant and wayward, since he himself is beset with weakness"* (Heb. 5:2). Can we have a better, more appropriate High Priest than the Lord Jesus – He is perfect for us: *"For we do not have a high priest who is unable to sympathize with our weaknesses, but one who in every respect has been tempted as we are, yet without sin"* (Heb. 4:15).

It is His humanity that makes Him our perfect High Priest as is indicated by the passage inserted between two of the references to the priesthood of Melchizedek: *"In the days of his flesh, Jesus offered up prayers and supplications, with loud cries and tears, to him who was able to save him from death, and he was heard because of his reverence. Although he was a son, he learned obedience through what he suffered. And being made perfect, he became the source of eternal salvation to all who obey him, being designated by God a high priest after the order of Melchizedek"* (Heb. 5:6–10).

In this letter there are plenty of verses that describe the complete identification of the Saviour with those He came to save. No one was ever more convinced of the humanity of Jesus than the writer of the Hebrew epistle.

HIS QUALIFICATIONS FOR OFFICE: 2. CALLED OF GOD

By the time of the advent of the Saviour, the office of Israel's High Priest had fallen into disrepute. It had, when inaugurated, been conditioned on the holder of the office being of the family of Aaron. Not only so, but the High Priest held the position for life – it passed to his son at his decease. But in the history of Israel, especially during the period between the Testaments, because of its political power, it was an office that was coveted by many who had neither the right nor the qualification to hold the post. There were some that bought it and others that took it by force. At the time of the ministry of the Messiah it was held by Caiaphas – branded by Christ as a thief and a robber. It had ceased to be the province of those who had been 'called of God'. Nevertheless, the 'call of God' remained one of the conditions that had to be met by anyone who was genuinely God's choice: *"no one takes this honour for himself, but only when called by God, just as Aaron was"* (Heb. 5:4). This certainly was the case with the Messiah: *"So also Christ did not exalt himself to be made a high priest, but was appointed by him who said to him, "You are my Son, today I have begotten you"; as he says also in another place, "You are a priest forever, after the order of Melchizedek""* (Heb. 5:5–6).

The quote from Psalm 2:7 *"The LORD has said to Me, 'You are My Son, Today I have begotten You, '"* is thought to refer to several events in the life and experience of the Messiah. Initially to His birth, then to His baptism and then subsequently and more directly to His resurrection: *"this he has fulfilled to us their children by raising Jesus, as also it is written in the second Psalm, 'You are my Son, today I have begotten you'"* (Acts 13:33).

All events were absolutely essential to the High Priestly office. The first event being the incarnation (see above); then secondly when He fully embraced His mission at His baptism; and thirdly where the first phase of the redemptive plan of God was complete and Christ was resurrected to take up His post in the presence of the Father in the most Holy Place.

HIS QUALIFICATIONS FOR OFFICE: 3. CONFIRMED BY AN OATH

The commissioning text that the author of Hebrews returns to is Psalm 110.4, *"The LORD has sworn and will not change his mind, "You are a priest forever after the order of Melchizedek""*, a text that makes mention of an oath. Those of the Levitical order of High Priest were inducted without an oath – so this is slightly unusual. So we ask the question, 'Why with an oath?' The answer is provided - *"This makes Jesus the guarantor of a better covenant"* (Heb. 7:22). This means He guarantees the terms of the covenant under which He operates. This covenant we have yet to consider – however we can state it is the 'New Covenant' which contains majestic spiritual blessings – described here as *"a better covenant"*. What is a guarantor? For many years the financial world in the U.K. operated a system of loans/mortgages which required a guarantor. The bank or similar institution would lend you money which you would be required to repay. However, if you defaulted the one who guaranteed your repayments could be called upon to make up the shortfall. Generally, it was expected that the guarantor would be able to ensure that the commitment you made with the bank was fully satisfied. This provided peace of mind to all parties, to those in the bank to assure them that the debt would be met in full, and to you, the borrower, that ultimately the debt would be paid and you would not suffer any distraining order. This is a very poor illustration of what the Bible is suggesting here, but it does identify the wondrous blessing that is ours under the New Covenant – that Jesus is our guarantor – that the terms of the covenant will be met to the satisfaction of both parties (God and believers). Since the oath assures us that He is a priest forever, there will never come a time when there will be a possibility of default and a withdrawal of mercy.

HIS QUALIFICATIONS FOR OFFICE: 4. A KING FOREVER

He speaks of the Melchizedekian priesthood in the most elevated of language displaying the highest regard for the office, listing qualifications necessary for the one called to serve, of such dignity, quality, and eternal value that no-one would think of arrogating this position to themselves (as was often the case with the Aaronic High Priest). This particular office of High Priest is only open to a king/priest; therefore, any called to serve would need to hold the position of sovereign as well as that of High Priest. He would be without beginning of days or end of life to be able to hold office for ever. He would need to 'neither slumber nor sleep' because he will never be off-duty but constantly interceding for those he represents.

The esteem in which the priesthood of Christ is held by the writer of Hebrews is evident by the space that He gives to the subject. It establishes the importance of the subject for him and, because he is writing under the inspiration of the Holy Spirit, for all believers. He quotes his proof text from Psalm 110:4 several times, and note the word 'forever':

"as he says also in another place, "You are a priest forever, after the order of Melchizedek"" (Heb. 5:6)

"being designated by God a high priest after the order of Melchizedek" (Heb. 5:10).

"where Jesus has gone as a forerunner on our behalf, having become a high priest forever after the order of Melchizedek" (Heb. 6:20).

"For it is witnessed of him, "You are a priest forever, after the order of Melchizedek"" (Heb. 7:17).

"but this one was made a priest with an oath by the one who said to him: "The Lord has sworn and will not change his mind, 'You are a priest forever'" (Heb. 7:21).

This is in contrast to the High Priest of the Aaronic order who was first required to offer sacrifice for his own sins before interceding for Israel. Not only so but even the best of them were subject to the consequences of sin, that is, they died. Let's examine how the Hebrew letter sets out the subject.

THE HISTORICAL EXAMPLE

While it is Psalms that provides the prophecy of the High Priesthood of Christ, it is an account in Genesis that supplies the type. The whole episode is sketched in three verses.

"And Melchizedek king of Salem brought out bread and wine. (He was priest of God Most High.) And he blessed him and said, "Blessed be Abram by God Most High, Possessor of heaven and earth; and blessed be God Most High, who has delivered your enemies into your hand!" And Abram gave him a tenth of everything" (Gen. 14:18–20).

The writer of the Hebrew epistle draws on this narrative to build on the prophecy of Ps.110.4. He uses the information provided as well as recognizing that there is certain data omitted. Accepting that, in the God-breathed account, both inclusions and omissions are important he offers a summary of the pertinent facts.

1. Melchizedek is a king as well as a priest.
2. His name means 'king of righteousness'.
3. He is king of Salem, that is, 'king of peace'.
4. Melchizedek blessed Abraham, that is, Abraham received a Melchizedekian blessing.
5. Abraham gave tithes to Melchizedek.
6. There is no mention of his decease. The writer to the Hebrews uses this omission to suggest that a High Priest of this order will never hand over the responsibility of the post to a successor.

Granted that Jesus is a priest of the order of Melchizedek, then these facts establish the supremacy of the priesthood of Christ over the priesthood of Aaron. The argument is presented in this fashion.

1. Abraham acknowledged the greatness of Melchizedek when he gave him "*a tenth of the spoils*" (Heb. 7:4).

2. Since Abraham was the father of the nation and Levi was yet unborn (which also applied to Aaron and his posterity) then the conclusion is - the Aaronic priesthood has to acknowledge the superiority of the Melchizedekian priesthood since the actions of father Abraham are considered to condition their respective positions ("*One might even say that Levi himself, who receives tithes, paid tithes through Abraham*" (Heb. 7:9)), and clearly, the lesser pays tithes to the greater.

To this are added further qualifications that could never have been fulfilled by Aaron, his sons or his descendants.

3. The holder needs to be a sovereign since it is an order of king/priests.

4. The holder needs to be eternal in his nature since he has to occupy the position, without interruption or relief, for ever.

"Now the point in what we are saying is this: we have such a high priest, one who is seated at the right hand of the throne of the Majesty in heaven, a minister in the holy places, in the true tent that the Lord set up, not man." (Heb. 8:1–2).

If Christ is a High Priest of the order of Melchizedek and the qualifications for that position are such that they are out of reach of the children of Adam, then it establishes beyond doubt His supremacy as the only High Priest who can intercede in the throne room of heaven. He has fulfilled the necessary conditions listed above, which are out of reach of all others.

He is of the tribe of Judah and was born 'king of the Jews'. He presented Himself to the nation as such. Although He was rejected by the nation's leaders and recommended for execution, it did not negate His position - His correct title was written in three languages on the cross – *"JESUS OF NAZARETH, KING OF THE JEWS"* (Matt.27:37; Mark 15:26; Luke 23:38; John 19:19). Subsequently exalted by His Father to the throne in heaven, He will yet occupy the throne of David in Jerusalem and reign from there (thus completing the type 'King of Salem').

Moreover, His priesthood can continue without interruption since He has been raised to die no more. *"He holds his priesthood permanently, because he continues forever"* (Heb. 7:24).

These superiorities reveal the efficiency of this order of priesthood. *"Consequently, he is able to save to the uttermost those who draw near to God through him, since he always lives to make intercession for them"* (Heb. 7:25). Everything necessary, for the acceptance by, and our approach to, our Father God, has been accomplished.

CHAPTER NINE

LIGHT FROM THE BOOK OF HEBREWS

THE MESSIAH – AND THE SUPERIOR SANCTUARY

The Temple, at the time of the Saviour and indeed at the date attributed to the writing of the letter to Hebrew Christians, was a magnificent building in a setting of intersecting courtyards bordered by impressive porches. Solomon had spared nothing in building the first Temple but it had been destroyed at the time of the Babylonian conquest of Israel. When some of the population returned after exile the Temple was rebuilt, but it was not of the same calibre as Solomon's glorious structure. But after Herod swore allegiance to the Roman cause and was inducted as 'king of the Jews' by the Roman senate, he initiated a program of building to rival that of Solomon. His hope was that he would be considered another Solomon and remembered as such. To this end he decided to replace the second Temple that occupied the Temple Mount with a larger, greater and more magnificent Sanctuary that would outshine even that of Solomon's. He began in 19 BC with the bulk of construction completed about 4 AD, although it was never finally completed until some decades after the death of the Lord Jesus.

Retaining walls were constructed around the Temple mount to provide a level building site of such size that it would not only be large enough for the footprint of the Sanctuary itself but also hold great public areas and be surrounded by porches where the public could shelter from sun and rain. The designated sacred Temple area was some 250 square yards and had five gates – two of which were main gates for the public to enter and exit (the Coponius Gate and a Huldah Gate) – another for the priests to enter and exit (the second Huldah Gate) – another gate towards the north of the Sanctuary through which they brought animals for sacrifice (the Tadi Gate) – and one more (the Shushan Gate) which was deemed an 'exit only' gate for the public, but which also served as the gate out of which they took the scapegoat on the Day of Atonement; the gate out of which they took the red heifer when occasion demanded it; and the gate out of which they took the carcasses of the Day of Atonement sin offerings to be burned 'outside the camp'.

The Sanctuary at the heart of the Temple area had a facing wall some 150 feet high in which was the door that led to the first room called the 'Holy Place'. This door was known as the Gate of the Golden Vine because its pillars were entwined with a vine made of gold. The second room of the Sanctuary was protected by a great curtain 60 feet high, thirty feet wide and almost four inches thick.

There were three pieces of furniture in the Holy Place; one was a seven-branch lampstand (the Menorah) which was made all of gold; and two others, the altar of incense and the table of showbread, which were made of wood that was then overlaid with gold. The second room, the Most Holy Place, should have had the sacred chest called 'the ark of the covenant' made of wood, overlaid with gold, with a lid made of gold. This lid, called 'the mercy seat' or sometimes the 'throne of God', was made of solid gold and had the form of a cherub worked into it at each end. Alas this remarkable piece of sacred furniture had been lost when the Temple had been looted by the Chaldeans. It had never been replaced, so the inner room of the Sanctuary was empty apart from the rock on which the ark used to stand.

In front of the Sanctuary was the court of priests and the court of prayer. The court of priests held the giant laver and the great altar, while the court of prayer was dominated by four towering Menorahs, 86 feet high. The pair of giant doors that separated these two courts was called the 'Gate of Nicanor'. In front of the Gate of Nicanor were the imposing semi-circular 'Fifteen Steps of Ascent'. At the eastern end of the court of prayer, also known as the court of women, was a heavily decorated gate called the 'Gate of the Pure and the Just'.

Altogether, the Temple building, the courts (of Israel, of the Israelites, of priests, of women, of Gentiles) with the surrounding porches would cover the playing area of six football pitches, and if you added the Herodian extensions it is suggested that it would cover an area that would take the footprint of Windsor Castle four times over. Considering the dimensions, materials and spiritual importance of the Jewish Temple, it is no surprise that the disciples marvelled at a sight which was considered one of the wonders of the world: *"And as he came out of the temple, one of his disciples said to him, "Look, Teacher, what wonderful stones and what wonderful buildings!""* (Mark 13:1; cf. Matt.24:1; Luke 21:5) Jesus Himself was happy to refer to the Temple compound as *"these great buildings?"* (Mark 13:2) But their time was coming to an end for Jesus said to them, *"You see all these, do you not? Truly, I say to you, there will not be left here one stone upon another that will not be thrown down"* (Matt. 24:2). He had previously prophesied regarding the city: *"For the days will come upon you, when your enemies will set up a barricade around you and surround you and hem you in on every side and tear you down to the ground, you and your children within you. And they will not leave one stone upon another in you, because you did not know the time of your visitation"* (Luke 19:43–44). The shadow, the model, was due to be put aside and replaced by the heavenly Sanctuary. In terms of dimensions the 'Superior Sanctuary' (the heavenly Sanctuary) was to be larger, greater, more imposing. This indicates that our High Priest officiates in *"the greater and more perfect tabernacle not made with hands, that is, not of this creation"* (Heb. 9:11 KJV).

And like the High Priest on the Day of Atonement, who entered the Most Holy Place, He entered the heavenly equivalent of the 'Most Holy Place', the throne room of God. But the similarity with the Aaronic High Priest ended there, for he did not attend on God with the blood of an animal sacrifice, but as the High Priest of the order of Melchizedek He presented His own precious blood.

To make his point the writer of the letter, in a few strokes, sketches the greatness of the Sanctuary in which Christ ministers. While the priests' court (where the sacrifice was effected) was on earth, the inner sanctum, the Holy of Holies of the real Sanctuary is in heaven, where the actual throne of God is located (not just in type as in the earthly Sanctuary but in reality). Jesus, our great High Priest, *"passed through the heavens"* (4:14) to reach it. This is more fully explained in chapter 9: *"For Christ has entered, not into holy places made with hands, which are copies of the true things, but into heaven itself, now to appear in the presence of God on our behalf"* (Heb. 9:24), and *"he entered once for all into **the holy places**, not by means of the blood of goats and calves but by means of his own blood, thus securing an eternal redemption"* (Heb. 9:12).

On the Day of Atonement, Israel's Aaronic High Priest went in and then came out. On the other hand, Jesus entered the throne room of heaven once and there remained. Not only remained but sat down (Heb. 1:3; 10:12), indicating His redemptive work was finished. Our understanding is, that **since atonement has been accomplished, the festival of Yom Kippur (Day of Atonement) is no longer needed**, although Israel, as a nation will not acknowledge that until brought to the end of their resources by 'Jacob's trouble'.

There is, of course, one major difference between the earthly Sanctuary and the heavenly; it reflects the difference between law and grace. The earthly Temple had a veil that was designed to keep everyone (except the High Priest) out. When Jesus declared *"it is finished"* the veil of the Temple was ripped from top to bottom. The heavenly Sanctuary begins as it were, with a torn veil, designed to encourage everyone to enter. In the heavenly sanctuary there is no impediment to our approach to the throne – we are encouraged to come into the presence of God: *"Therefore, brothers, since we have confidence to enter the holy places by the blood of Jesus, by the new and living way that he opened for us through the curtain, that is, through his flesh, and since we have a great priest over the house of God, **let us draw near** with a true heart in full assurance of faith"* (Heb. 10:19–22). The heavenly Sanctuary is designed to welcome all believers who bring with them nothing more than *"a true heart in full assurance of faith"*.

This suggests that the furniture of the Holy Place that aided the worship of Israel is also no longer needed. The Menorah that provided the light while they performed their duties as priests, the bread that spoke of communion and the altar of incense that aided their prayers, have each been replaced. The Spirit of God now provides all the light we need and He aids our prayers when we do not know how to pray as we aught. The remembrance meal of bread and wine is often and quite correctly termed 'communion'. All these are available to every Christian, which is just another way of speaking of the universal priesthood of all believers.

What is emphasized here is: the accoutrements of the law have gone because they are no longer needed. There is no Temple so there can be no place to sacrifice the Passover lamb and therefore no proper Passover celebration. With no Temple there is no place to bring the firstfruits of the harvest and therefore there can be no celebration of the Feast of Tabernacles. It is not as if this should make us sad. It is in accordance with God's purposes. It is the age of grace and the building that personified the law is properly gone. *"Our God is in the heavens; he does all that he pleases"* (Psalm 115:3).

CHAPTER TEN

LIGHT FROM THE BOOK OF HEBREWS

THE MESSIAH AND THE SUPERIOR COVENANT

FUNCTIONING UNDER A BETTER COVENANT

But if there is a new order of priest functioning in a different sanctuary then it must be on the authority of a new covenant. *"For when there is a change in the priesthood, there is necessarily a change in the law as well"* (Heb. 7:12). This is sound reasoning. Clearly, Jesus is not going to elevate the Mosaic covenant by becoming its greatest and most distinguished High Priest. This is for several reasons, the main one being that the Mosaic Covenant was a covenant of works – and this will not suit a dispensation of grace. Not only would it not be fit for purpose in this present age, but would be a positive hindrance (as is being demonstrated by those who wish to resurrect elements of it). This meanss that it could not be left intact alongside the New Covenant – it had to be removed. Paul, speaking of the law as a wall of separation, declared that Jesus demolished it – reduced it to rubble – took it away. *"For he ... has broken down in his flesh the dividing wall of hostility **by abolishing the law of commandments expressed in ordinances**"* (Eph. 2:14–15).

No – under this new High Priest there is no need to return to the Mosaic economy. It has been *"set aside"*. And for good reason – according to the writer, it was *"weak and useless ... it made nothing perfect"*. *"On the other hand"*, in this new dispensation *"a better hope is introduced, through which we draw near to God"* (Heb. 7:18–19). We are encouraged to look forward and not imitate Lot's wife and look back. In looking back, you are in danger of ending up petrified.

The argument of Hebrews is that with the advent of the New Covenant the Mosaic Covenant was of no further use, that is, it is obsolete. *"In speaking of a new covenant, he makes the first one obsolete. And what is becoming obsolete and growing old is ready to vanish away"* (Heb. 8:13). Since the dating of the Hebrew letter is just before the siege of Jerusalem by the Romans, it is sometimes thought that *"ready to vanish away"* points to the destruction of the Temple. Certainly, with its destruction, the Mosaic sacerdotal system of worship physically ended. It had no ground on which to operate – no Aaronic High Priest, no functioning sanctuary, no Day of Atonement sacrifices. In other words, the heart of the old covenant system was torn out. Because of this, the Hebrew people have a very limited choice – take Jesus as the Messiah and High Priest and be reconciled to God, or reject Him and His atoning work and be banished from the presence of God forever, suffering eternal consequences.

But why would they want to return to the Old Covenant? Clearly, the writer is offering the assurance that the New is better than the Old and that it would be folly to go from the superior (the New Covenant) to the inferior (the Old Covenant). *"But as it is, Christ has obtained a ministry that is as much more excellent than the old as the covenant he mediates is better, since it is enacted on better promises. For if that first covenant had been faultless, there would have been no occasion to look for a second"* (Heb. 8:6–7). The first covenant (as the law of Moses is labelled in Hebrews) was flawed (*"for if that first covenant had been faultless, there would have been no occasion to look for a second"* (Heb. 8:7)). It was declared to be faulty because no individual Jew could keep it (until Jesus, Son of man, came). Peter, the apostle to the Jews, acknowledged its defects when he said it was a burden *"neither our fathers nor we have been able to bear?"* (Acts 15:10). No – the only hope for the Jewish people is in the covenant of grace, the superior covenant, where God commits to its fulfilment.

So the New Covenant is different – radically different, it is *"not like the covenant that I made with their fathers on the day when I took them by the hand to bring them out of the land of Egypt"* (Heb. 8:9). Can we identify the main differences? Initially it must be observed that it is not a two party covenant as was the Old Covenant. At Sinai Israel undertook to obey, not only the Decalogue but a multitude of other requirements: *"All that the LORD has spoken we will do"* (Exod. 19:8), they said. But this fresh covenant is a covenant of grant - there are no obligations (save one) placed on those who choose to shelter under its provisions – God is committed to save, keep and change them if they turn to Him through their Messiah. The terms are spelt out in detail: *"For this is the covenant that **I will** make with the house of Israel after those days, declares the Lord: **I will** put my laws into their minds, and write them on their hearts, and **I will** be their God, and they shall be my people. And they shall not teach, each one his neighbour and each one his brother, saying, 'Know the Lord,' for they shall all know me, from the least of them to the greatest. For **I will** be merciful toward their iniquities, and **I will** remember their sins no more"'* (Heb. 8:10–12). Note the repetition of the commitment of God, *"I will ... I will ... I will ... I will ... I will."*

The unyielding character of the Law was reflected in its mode of delivery. It was written on stone! However, the covenant of grace is written on tablets of flesh, that is, the human heart: *"I will ... write them on their hearts"* (Heb. 8:10) God says. The one is external and requires constant dedication and unending energy to comply, whereas the New Covenant simply requires a willingness to let God provide the enabling. The importance of 'letting go and letting God' can be illustrated as follows. There was a church in France that was blessed with an organ that could produce music in praise of God. One day when the church organist was playing (not very well, it might be said) a stranger entered the church and asked to play the instrument. He was refused – it seemed the church organist was a little protective of the fine, old organ. The stranger asked a second and even a third time until he was granted permission. Then when he began to play, that organ produced music sweeter and more melodious than it had ever produced before. The sound rose and filled every nook and cranny of the great branching roof – it might have been thought to have awakened sleeping choirs of angels – certainly the music was in praise of the Creator. When the stranger finished playing the church organist pressed him – 'Who are you? Who are you?' he asked. 'I'm Mendelssohn' was the reply, to which the church organist responded brokenly, 'to think that I nearly refused Mendelssohn the use of my instrument'. A greater tragedy would be for any to refuse God the use of their instrument, for God can make music out of our lives that is beyond all expectation. To repeat, God says: *"I will put my laws into their minds, and write them on their hearts, and I will be their God, and they shall be my people. And they shall not teach, each one his neighbour and each one his brother, saying, 'Know the Lord,' for they shall all know me, from the least of them to the greatest. For I will be merciful toward their iniquities, and I will remember their sins no more'"* (Heb. 8:10–12).

The practical difficulty that had to be overcome is obvious - the Jewish nation had been under the Mosaic economy for such a considerable time. They could not envisage a day when the law would not apply. Nevertheless, one fact is clear – it was not designed to be in place eternally. It had a built-in weakness; it was only *"a shadow of the good things to come instead of the true form of these realities"*, therefore *"it can never, by the same sacrifices that are continually offered every year, make perfect those who draw near"* (Heb. 10:1). It was to cease when it accomplished its main purpose. What was its main purpose and when would it cease? Paul asked and answered these very questions in Galatians: *"Why then the law? It was added because of transgressions, **until the offspring should come** to whom the promise had been made"* (Gal. 3:19). It was added … until the offspring (that is the 'seed of the woman', Christ) should come. Christ has come and the age of law is over! The Bible is very clear – the age of law has been superseded by the age of grace, and the instrument of covenant on which this age is founded is simply called the New Covenant.

IS THERE A CONNECTION BETWEEN THE OLD COVENANT AND THE NEW?

There is! The Old was the shadow of the New. It promised better things. Those better things arrived with the day of grace. *"Christ appeared as a high priest of **the good things that have come**"* (Heb. 9:11). *"He is the mediator of a new covenant, so that those who are called may receive the promised eternal inheritance, since a death has occurred **that redeems them from the transgressions committed under the first covenant**"* (Heb. 9:15). The writer's logic is evident – those who were under the law but have now acknowledged the person and work of the Messiah have been set free by the death of the Messiah. Having been set free, the exhortation is: do not now return to your former bondage. *"For freedom Christ has set us free; stand firm therefore, and do not submit again to a yoke of slavery"* (Gal. 5:1).

The superiority of the mechanism of the New Covenant over that of the Old covenant is described under another *"how much more"*. *"For if the blood of goats and bulls, and the sprinkling of defiled persons with the ashes of a heifer, sanctify for the purification of the flesh,* **how much more** *will the blood of Christ, who through the eternal Spirit offered himself without blemish to God, purify our conscience* **from dead works** *to serve the living God"* (Heb. 9:13–14). What is implied by this text is – the redemption that Christ provides releases us from all attempts to provide other means aimed at achieving divine approval.

CHAPTER ELEVEN

LIGHT FROM THE BOOK OF HEBREWS

THE MESSIAH - THE SUPERIOR SACRIFICE

The Bible declares that the death of Christ was a sacrifice of limitless value – it would crown all previous sacrifices. Those who acknowledge it and shelter under its canopy of benefit will escape the wrath of God, gain entrance to the presence of God and be placed under the protection of God. In contrast, the offerings under the Mosaic covenant are declared to have been ultimately ineffective to deal with humanity's sinfulness – priests stood *"ministering daily and offering repeatedly the same sacrifices, which can never take away sins"*. But the superior sacrifice presented by our superior High Priest has produced superior results: *"But this Man, after He had offered **one sacrifice for sins forever**, sat down at the right hand of God, from that time waiting till His enemies are made His footstool. **For by one offering He has perfected forever those who are being sanctified"** (Heb. 10:11–14).

The execution of Jesus only makes sense in the priestly culture of Israel since it was a sacrifice for sin, and a sacrifice that perfected all previous sacrifices.

1. It was a sacrifice of the highest purity and value being the voluntary offer of the life of the only innocent man that ever lived, who was also the beloved Son of God.

2. It was a sacrifice that was itself complete, needing no repetition and no further offerings to supplement it.

3. It was a sacrifice that had unlimited merit and was effective for all who wished to shelter under its protection.

4. It was an effective sacrifice in that it removed sin, instead of just covering it.

5. It was a sacrifice that has proved itself to be the most beneficial, providing access to the living God in the heavenly throne room, from where grace to help in time of need was available.

THE QUALITY OF THE SUPERIOR SACRIFICE – THE DEITY OF CHRIST

On Calvary the sacrifice for sin was of limitless and eternal value since it was the Person in whom is eternal life with all the attributes and qualities of deity—the Son of God. The opening of the Hebrew epistle sets the tone, using descriptors of the Messiah that can only refer to the eternal second person of the Godhead. *"Long ago, at many times and in many ways, God spoke to our fathers by the prophets, but in these last days he has spoken to us by his Son, whom he appointed the heir of all things, through whom also he created the world.* **He is the radiance of the glory of God and the exact imprint of his nature,** *and he upholds the universe by the word of his power"* (Heb. 1:1–3).

The Son is *"the radiance of God's glory and the exact representation of his being"*. Each word throbs with deity. *"He is the radiance of God's glory"*, specifically the Shekinah glory (everything that is true of the Father in terms of glory is also true of the Son). This emphasizes His co-essence, not only co-equal but the very outshining of the Father in terms of glory. The eternal light which emanates from the Father, which would be too much for mortals to bear, also emanates from the Son. He is *"the exact imprint of His* (God's) *nature"*. The writer is struggling to find words to express the mystery that is the Godhead, yet produces phrases which can have no other explanation than the deity of the Son is exactly the same as the deity of the Father, that is, everything that is true of God the Father is true of God the Son. All the attributes of the Father are in the Son exactly, completely, perfectly, literally, expressly, in every respect.

There is no question among Christians about the deity of either the Father or the Spirit. Similarly, I would suggest there should no shadow over the deity of the Son. But when He embraced the mission of becoming the Messiah of Israel; of accepting the office of High Priest of the order of Melchizedek; of embracing the necessity of offering His life in payment for the sin of humanity; it produced in the minds of many a conflict of harmonizing His deity and humanity. However, the deity of the incarnate Son is asserted in the Bible as fully and as clearly in every particular as is the deity of the Father or the Spirit. Heb.1.8: *"But to the Son He says: "Your throne, O God, is forever and ever; A sceptre of righteousness is the sceptre of Your kingdom"*. This and other verses teach that Jesus is both God and man.

THE QUALITY OF THE SUPERIOR SACRIFICE – THE PURITY OF CHRIST

Earlier in the chapter we suggested that the superiority of the sacrifice partly rested in the fact that it was the voluntary offer of the life of the only innocent man that ever lived. While it is generally necessary to give more space to the deity of Christ, as we have, we must in no way overlook the purity of His person. His humanity was as sinless as His deity. As unfallen man, the seed of the woman, and born of a virgin, He was not only free from a sin nature, but sinless as to His speech, actions, motives and thoughts. This was necessary: *"For it was fitting for us to have such a high priest, **holy, innocent, undefiled, separated from sinners** and exalted above the heavens"* (Heb. 7:26, NASB).

Here the suitability of the Messiah for His priestly ministry is described, four words capturing His purity.

1. Jesus is *"holy"*, a word describing his inner character and in the immediate context suggests sinlessness. The word carries the idea of piety and inner purity.

2. This Jesus is also *"innocent"*, that is, free from evil or guile.

3. *"Undefiled"* means untainted by sin, that is, not soiled by any legal or moral pollution. The writer is pointing out that Jesus is free from anything that would in any way defile, prohibit, or disqualify him from priestly service. While this was *"fitting"*, that is, part of the job description of a High Priest of the calibre needed to present an offering of the highest value and the greatest efficacy, such holiness and purity

are also essential elements in the One whose life is to be a *"ransom for many"*. Any taint of sin would have invalidated the offering.

4. Jesus is also described as *"separated from sinners"*, a phrase which taken with the preceding statements must mean moral separation.

THE EFFICIENCY OF THE SUPERIOR SACRIFICE

It was a sacrifice that was itself complete, needing no repetition and no further offerings to supplement it. It was once, for all. The Greek words 'hapax' (translated 'once') and 'ephapax' (also translated 'once') are used 6 times in the Hebrew letter (7.27; 9.12; 9.26; 9.28; 10.2; 10.10) as also 'mian' (translated 'one') (10.12) and 'miai' (also translated 'one') (10.14). They emphasize His single sacrifice; typically, *"now, **once** at the end of the ages, He has appeared to put away sin by the sacrifice of Himself. And as it is appointed for men to die once, but after this the judgment, so Christ was offered **once** to bear the sins of many"* (9:26–28).

The priests repeated their work because it was ineffective, but Christ does not need to repeat His, because it was effective. The 'once and for all' nature of Christ's sacrifice is seen in the fact that the Aaronic priest stood while serving, while Christ sat down at God's right hand because His offering was finished. It had been fully accepted and no further offering was required. His atoning work was done, as declared: *"Now where there is remission of these, there is no longer an offering for sin"* (Heb. 10.18).

"Done is the work that saves,

once and for ever done;

Finished the righteousness

that clothes the unrighteous one".

(Horatius Bonar)

The New Covenant requires a sacrifice of this magnitude because its terms are so all-encompassing; *"This is the covenant that I will make with them after those days, says the LORD: I will put My laws into their hearts, and in their minds I will write them. "* To this is added: *"Their sins and their lawless deeds I will remember no more"* before the text regarding the finality of the work of Christ: *"Now where there is remission of these, there is no longer an offering for sin"* (Heb. 10:16–18). This spells out the divine guarantee that, for those under the New Covenant, the subject of their sins and iniquities will never be raised again. Here is God's promise of eternal forgiveness. This kind of remission of sin requires a sacrifice of such efficiency that places a New Covenant believer under the beneficent protection of the Father eternally. The superior sacrifice is such an offering. Nevertheless, the statement: *"Now where there is remission of these, there is no longer an offering for sin"* calls for a further explanation. The word for *'offering'* (prosphora) has two meanings:

First it is used to identify that which is brought before God - a sacrifice, an offering. That the death of Christ was such an offering was stated by Isaiah (Isa. 53:10-12) and confirmed by the New Testament writers (Eph. 5:2; Heb. 9:14).

However, there is a second meaning of the word when it refers to the act of offering or presenting a sacrifice. The text of Hebrews 10:14 (*"For by one offering He has perfected forever those who are being sanctified"*) calls for this second meaning also. While the death of Christ need not be repeated – it was 'once, for all', the writer is also asserting that the whole Mosaic system of animal sacrifices for sin has finished. The kind of remission gained by the sacrifice of the pure Lamb of God is such that the Mosaic sacerdotal regime can cease – *"there is no longer an offering for sin"*, that is, there is no further need for a sacrifice for sin. Indeed, the writer has already implied that it will be forcibly stopped in his near future.[32]

The efficiency of the superior sacrifice is also seen in that it removed sin, instead of just covering it. The author of Hebrews writes: *"how much more shall the blood of Christ, who through the eternal Spirit offered Himself without spot to God, cleanse your conscience from dead works to serve the*

---

[32] Cf. Heb. 8:13

living God?" (Heb. 9:14) The cleansing power of the blood of Christ sanctifies, not in some external, ceremonial way, but in reality. It purifies the conscience, and provides full and eternal forgiveness. This is described as eternal redemption (Heb. 9:12); the cleansing of the conscience (Heb. 9:13,14); the removal of sin (Heb. 9:26); the perfecting of the worshipper (Heb. 10:1,14); sanctification (Heb. 10:10,14); and the forgiveness of sins and lawless acts (Heb. 10:18). Nothing need be added, indeed nothing can be added, to the sacrifice of the Lord Jesus, to improve our standing with our Heavenly Father.

CHAPTER TWELVE

SOME FINAL REMARKS REGARDING THE AGE OF LAW

The sum of what has been said is that we need to recognize which covenant applies to us and which dispensation we live in. Before we finish perhaps we should sketch out the main features of the age of law and formulate a response.

THE GIVING OF THE LAW

The giving of the law was at the time of the exodus from Egypt when the nation was trying to recover from an extended period of slavery. They were ill-prepared for nationhood so God set about providing them with leadership, and a moral and ethical code by which to live, and government that would produce discipline and order. The nation was to be ordered as a theocracy. The code which would mould them would be issued from the throne of heaven. The law, with its mixture of commands and regulations governing social and religious behaviour, was designed to train the nation in holiness and to provide a vehicle by which Israel could fellowship with their God. They would not be an end in themselves – they would be preparatory for a further outworking of the purposes of their divine Author when God's champion, the seed of the woman,[33] would come to defeat Satan and redeem Adam's posterity. At Sinai, the mount of God, Moses was called into the divine presence, where an offer of a covenant was made. *"And Moses went up to God, and the LORD called to him from the mountain, saying, "Thus you shall say to the house of Jacob, and tell the children of Israel: 'You have seen what I did to the Egyptians, and how I bore you on eagles' wings and brought you to Myself. Now therefore, if you will indeed obey My voice and keep My covenant, then you shall be a special treasure to Me above all*

---

[33] Gen. 3:15

people; for all the earth is Mine. And you shall be to Me a kingdom of priests and a holy nation.'" (Exod. 19:3-6) To this offer they unanimously replied, *"All that the LORD has spoken we will do."* (Exod. 19:8)

But it would be necessary for every individual Israelite to understand that these regulations were authored by the LORD and not by Moses. Therefore, the initial communication of the law of God would be by direct communication from above. The Decalogue on which the law was to be based would first be audibly communicated by God Himself, then written with His finger on tablets of stone while attended by some of nature's most awesome and violent events. The unfolding drama that was the offering of the covenant was witnessed by more than two million. Thunders, lightening and earthquakes attended the descent of the LORD on to the pinnacle of Horeb. With such evident manifestations of the presence and mind of God, everyone was clear about one thing - this code was to be non-negotiable – there would be no modifying of its requirements: either obey it, or face the Omnipotent and explain why! The code under which they would serve would teach them to differentiate between holy and unholy, between clean and unclean. So Israel, from the dark womb of Egypt, was brought to birth as a nation, and called the firstborn of the LORD.[34] It is clear that the Mosaic covenant was established between Israel and the LORD. No other nations are involved. No other combination of peoples is involved. Moses repeats this truth, when he addresses the nation at the end of his life. *"For what great nation is there that has God so near to it, as the LORD our God is to us, for whatever reason we may call upon Him? And what great nation is there that has such statutes and righteous judgments as are in all this law which I set before you this day?"* (Deut. 4:7,8) This is repeated in the 'writings'; *"He declares His word to Jacob, His statutes and His judgments to Israel. **He has not dealt thus with any nation**; And as for His judgments, they have not known them. Praise the LORD!"* (Ps. 147:19,20)

---

[34] Exod. 4:22

The terms of the Mosaic Covenant have been examined and analysed over centuries, and Jewish legal experts have ordered and codified it in such a way that the nation could understand its requirements and obey its precepts. The need to understand and obey it arose from the fact that there were blessings offered for obedience and curses threatened for disobedience, as vocalized by Moses himself. *"Behold, I set before you today a blessing and a curse: the blessing, if you obey the commandments of the LORD your God which I command you today; and the curse, if you do not obey the commandments of the LORD your God"*. (Deut. 11:26-28)

TREASURED POSSESSION

The giving of the law, went hand-in-hand with the offer of a special relationship. *"Now therefore, if you will indeed obey my voice and keep my covenant, you shall be my treasured possession among all peoples, for all the earth is mine; and you shall be to me a kingdom of priests and a holy nation"* (Exod. 19:5–6). *"Treasured possession"* is 'segulah' in Hebrew, the private property of a king, as distinct from that used for public purposes, as with David.[35] Israel was to be God's *"treasured possession"*. This particular and peculiar relationship is referred to again in Deuteronomy. *"For you are a people holy to the LORD your God. The LORD your God has chosen you to be a people for his treasured possession, out of all the peoples who are on the face of the earth"* (Deut. 7:6).[36]

KINGDOM OF PRIESTS

"And you shall be to me a kingdom of priests" (Exod.19.6). This implies more than just holding a priestly caste – more like each and all members of the nation being considered together as a priestly entity. Indeed, later Jewish tradition understood it as such, converting it from a promise to a

---

[35] 1 Chron. 29:3

[36] See also Deut. 14:2 and 26:18

responsibility (noblesse oblige), and requiring the whole population to live by the same code of holiness as the priests.

A HOLY NATION

All members of the Hebrew race to discern between holy and unholy, between clean and unclean,[37] and live accordingly. The offer of this special relationship on the basis of obedience to the law was universally accepted (Exod. 19:8).

THE LAW

The law itself was in three sections - commandments, judgments and ordinances. It provided a code of conduct and rule of law that brought order and structure to allow them to function, not as twelve separate tribes, but as one nation, as well as providing the sacerdotal organization in which their relationship with the LORD might flourish. The rule of reception for those under law were simple: all males had to be circumcised and everyone (men and women) had to be Torah-observant.

COMMANDMENTS

At the heart of this binding agreement are the commandments and the heart of the commandments is the Decalogue[38] which later gave rise to the Sh'ma[39]. These were famously summarized by the Messiah. When asked, *"Teacher, which is the great commandment in the law?"* Jesus answered, *'You shall love the Lord your God with all your heart, with all your soul, and with all your mind.' This is the first and great commandment. And the*

---

[37] Lev.10.10

[38] Exod. 20:1-17

[39] Deut. 6:4 ff

second is like it: 'You shall love your neighbour as yourself.' On these two commandments hang all the law ..." (Matt. 22:36-40).

JUDGMENTS

The second category, coming under the general description 'judgments', deals with social requirements. (Exod.21.1-23.3) It begins, *"Now these are the judgments which you shall set before them"*. Examples include, *"If you buy a Hebrew servant, he shall serve six years; and in the seventh he shall go out free and pay nothing. If he comes in by himself, he shall go out by himself; if he comes in married, then his wife shall go out with him. If his master has given him a wife, and she has borne him sons or daughters, the wife and her children shall be her master's, and he shall go out by himself."* (Ex 21:2-4) There are regulations concerning the punishment to be inflicted for the taking of a life deliberately, and the compensation to be paid for the taking of a life accidentally. They not only deal with the loss and impairing of human life, but also animal life. This is given importance since the nation would continue to be an agricultural society. Also promulgated are detailed laws dealing with stealing, cheating and telling untruths; as also are encouragements to deal kindly with strangers and the poor. These laws are designed to produce a nation that would reflect the righteousness and mercy of the LORD.

ORDINANCES

The third category is 'ordinances'. These regulate the worship of Israel, that is, the activities of the priesthood and the ordering of the calendar to include annual festivals.[40] The 'ordinances' section includes regulations to do with the consecration of a priesthood, the service in the Sanctuary and the description of permitted offerings.

---

[40] Exod.25.1 to 31.18

THE LAW'S ACCOMPLISHMENTS

The imposing of this magnificent organisational and educational system on Israel must be considered one of the finest blessings that God could have granted to any people. He had purposed that they should be a mediatorial nation, revealing to humanity the principles of righteousness and mercy. There was a cost to the nation, but it was outweighed by the special relationship they had with the God of heaven. Israel's legal and sacrificial culture would protect and prosper them for millennia.

God's purposes in putting Israel under the discipline of law were gloriously accomplished.

1. It separated Israel from the other nations. This was required for several reasons, the largest of which was to train them to provide the environment for the incarnation where the Son of God could live a righteous life without being an object of ridicule.

2. It trained Israel to understand the righteousness of God and the exceeding sinfulness of sin.

3. They came to understand that they could never achieve by works the standard of righteousness that God required (they were given the sacrificial system as a vehicle to entreat for the mercy of God).

4. The sacrificial system taught them the principles of substitution, which would be vital for the wider redemption to be accomplished by the Redeemer.

5. They were given all they needed to be able to recognise God's mysterious champion, the 'seed of the woman', when He arrived.

Such are the main features of the 'age of law'. For those that were born under this regime it was all-encompassing. It affected everything – diet, study, work, dress, marriage, worship. There were no half measures – it was all or nothing. As a system of government designed to shape and fashion a nation it was effective – probably the greatest that has been evidenced anywhere at any time. Such an imposing and excellent regime should only yield to that which is better. The writer of the Hebrew epistle argues *"that which is better"* was promised under law and arrived with the coming of the Messiah. Those that embrace the new order will testify it is many times better. Those that have identified themselves with the crucified Saviour have been granted eternal life, the presence and help of the Spirit of God each day, and an eternal home prepared for them.

CHAPTER THIRTEEN

SOME FINAL REMARKS REGARDING THE AGE OF GRACE

THE EMPHASIS IN THE AGE OF GRACE

With the change of dispensation (from law to grace) the rules of reception changed. Under the New Covenant only those who are *"born again"* can be members of the 'ekklesia' (John 3:7). This signalled a sea change in all of heaven's dealings with humankind. The principles of righteousness that govern His relationship with humanity did not change because He does not change. He is the Immutable. But there came a time when animal sacrifices that expressed a plea for mercy could no longer be acceptable. At the time when the nation was mature and conditions were appropriate God sent His Son, His only Son Whom He loved, to crown the sacerdotal culture of Israel and be the sacrifice to provide meaning to all previous sacrifices. After the death of Christ things could never be the same again. The age of grace had begun. As John reminds us *"the law was given through Moses; grace ... came through Jesus Christ."* (John 1:17). From then on, the only plea for mercy that would be attended to by God is the one based on the sacrifice of the Lamb of God.

The immediate followers of the Messiah were commissioned to advertise the new regime, *"Go therefore and make disciples of all nations, baptizing them in the name of the Father and of the Son and of the Holy Spirit, teaching them to observe all that I have commanded you. And behold, I am with you always, to the end of the age"* (Matt. 28:19–20).

Peter began it on the day of Pentecost – when asked by those of Jerusalem who were aware of the crucifixion, what must we do? Peter replied, *"Repent and be baptized every one of you in the name of Jesus Christ for the forgiveness of your sins, and you will receive the gift of the Holy Spirit"* (Acts 2:38). And then later: *"there is salvation in no one else, for there is no other name under heaven given among men by which we must be saved"* (Acts 4:12). And at the Jerusalem council: *"But we believe that we will be saved through the grace of the Lord Jesus"* (Acts 15:11) Peter, apostle to the Jews, was saved by grace – Hallelujah!

Paul and Barnabas continued it: to the Philippian jailer who asked *"Sirs, what must I do to be saved?"* they answered, *"Believe in the Lord Jesus, and you will be saved, you and your household""* (Acts 16:30–31).

DOES GRACE DO AWAY WITH LAW?

What should be the attitude of New Covenant believers to those parts of the Mosaic Covenant described as 'commandments'? Without question - they should obey them! All that is included in the Decalogue (except the commandment regarding the Sabbath), has been repeated in one form or another in the New Testament and is therefore binding on New Covenant believers. However, there is a major difference. They are not external edicts as such but rather spiritual principles written on the heart and worked out in the life. There are no curses offered for disobedience. *"There is therefore now no condemnation for those who are in Christ Jesus"* (Rom. 8:1). We have been set free. James spoke of it: *"For it has seemed good to the Holy Spirit and to us to lay on you no greater burden than these requirements: that you abstain from what has been sacrificed to idols, and from blood, and from what has been strangled, and from sexual immorality. If you keep yourselves from these, you will do well."* (Acts 15:28–29). Paul expands it a little: *"the righteous requirement of the law"* are *"fulfilled in us, who walk not according to the flesh but according to the Spirit."* (Rom. 8:1–4)

It is evident that the principles of justice, mercy, hospitality and beneficence still apply but not because of outward constraints. Believers fulfil the appeals of Scripture because they have the Spirit of Christ. The letter of the law that was imposed on Israel does not apply. We do not need regulations regarding slavery or the mixing of crops; and we certainly do not punish people by stoning them. The external law is not applicable and any return to these externals can only be retrogressive.

But as regards to that section called 'ordinances' which deal with the sacrificial system, it would seem to this writer that this section, in particular, no longer applies. The sacrifice needed to satisfy the righteousness of God and quench the 'wrath of God' has been offered *"once for all"* (Heb. 7:27; 9:12; 10:10). Even for Israel it is no longer needed – conveniently so since she has no Temple or priesthood.

CONCLUSION

At the heart of our enquiry has been a comparison of the Mosaic and New Covenants. Which has the pre-eminence? We have suggested that the New Covenant is later, greater, current and permanent; the Mosaic was earlier, lesser, temporary and has vanished away.[41] The Hebrew epistle made a comparison of the main elements of both and confirms this assessment. We began by asking three questions. As we conclude we ask them again but in reverse order.

Question 3: *"Is obedience to the law of Moses still required of members of the Jewish race?"*

Answer: Absolutely not! There is no law-keeping that can supplement the sacrifice of the Messiah to make anyone acceptable (or 'more acceptable') to God. In fact, with the destruction of the Temple it is impossible to comply with the demands of the law. There is now no place for legal sacrifices, no priesthood, no place to celebrate the 'pilgrim' feasts, no place to bring freewill offerings, and no place to offer thanksgiving to the God of heaven for His mercy and His bounty. Furthermore, there is no Temple for members of the Jewish race to 'look toward' as they pray (as identified in Solomon's dedication prayer in 2 Chron. 6). No – the Age of the law has expired and all people (whether Jew or Gentile) must come to God on the basis of the superior sacrifice (Christ) offered by the superior High Priest (of the order of Melchizedek) and embrace the New Covenant. This, of course, does not remove the need for those of Jewish pedigree to remember the exodus and the birth of the nation with gratitude. In the culture of Israel, it is an event that will always have a special place. But the redemption of the nation (when every living Jew will be brought under the New Covenant) is yet to take place. It will happen at the end of the Tribulation period when Israel's leaders will finally call for the nation to repent of their sins, especially the rejection and execution of their Messiah. They will be brought to seek God's

---

[41] Heb. 8:13

mercy on the ground that "*he was pierced for our transgressions; he was crushed for our iniquities*" (Isaiah 53:5).

Question 2: "*If you are a Christian how do you relate to the law of Moses?*"

Answer: While acknowledging the value of the principles of righteousness and the code of ethics enshrined in the law of Moses, believers can rejoice in the fact that the Messiah has set them free from its multitude of regulations. They are able to listen to the voice of the Spirit of God which speaks loud and clear: "*You shall love the Lord your God with all your heart and with all your soul and with all your mind ... and ... your neighbour as yourself*" (Matt. 22:37–39).

But what of those who wish to offer thanks to the Lord of Hosts by recognising the contribution that the law has made to the accomplishment of their salvation? May they celebrate the Jewish festivals, albeit in a limited manner? For those dedicated believers who simply wish to show their devotion to YHWH we must sound a word of warning. Since it is impossible to fulfil the law's requirements as laid down in the T'nach, even the best effort offered will be considerably less than perfect. Under Torah regulations this would disqualify it from being acceptable. Passover cannot be celebrated without the slaying of the Lamb. Tabernacles cannot be celebrated without preceding it by the Day of Atonement, etc. Any celebrations that fall short of the Torah regulations should not be attempted. As James reminds us: "*For whoever keeps the whole law but fails in one point has become accountable for all of it*" (James 2:10) and Isaiah reminds us "*all our righteous deeds are like a polluted garment*" (Isaiah 64:6).

Question 1: "*Do you need to be a Jew to become a Christian?*"

Answer: According to the determination of the Jerusalem council in Acts 15 there are no conditions arising from the Mosaic covenant that need to be fulfilled by a Gentile before they can become a child of God. This confirmed the gospel that Paul preached, which he declared he had received by revelation from the Messiah Himself.

Not only are there no conditions arising from the Mosaic covenant that need to be fulfilled before an individual can become a child of God, but there are also no conditions arising from the law of Moses that need to be observed subsequent to conversion, although much that is expected in Christian behaviour under the New Covenant was similarly expected of those 'under law'.

Other Titles by Bryan W. Sheldon

The Miracles of the Messiah

'The Miracles of the Messiah' is an examination of the miracles (signs) that Jesus performed to support His claim that He was the true Messiah of Israel. It will ask and answer the questions; 'How did the nation's leaders investigate His claims and decide to reject them, in spite of the overwhelming evidence provided?' and 'How did Jesus respond to their decision?'

161 pages: Published by Gospel Folio Press, Port Colborne (2006):
ISBN: 1897117396

The Messiah and the Feasts of Israel

Part of the importance of the Feasts of the Lord in the calendar of the Hebrew nation is as a prophetic timetable of God's redemptive plan. Jesus died at Passover, was buried at the Feast of Unleavened Bread, rose at the Feast of Firstfruits and dispensed the Holy Spirit at the Feast of Weeks. The book also examines the Autumn feasts whose significance is yet to be fulfilled when He returns.

163 pages: Published by Gospel Folio Press, Port Colborne (2007)
ISBN: 9781897117590

The Messiah and the Covenants of Israel

This book is an examination of the Covenants of Israel, especially the New Covenant, since it is the rock on which the blessing of the Church is founded. The author offers an answer to the question, 'How can the Church enjoy the blessing of the New Covenant when it was declared to be for the nation of Israel?'

181 pages: Published by Gospel Folio Press, Port Colborne (2007) ISBN: 9781926765105

The Messiah and the Priesthood of Israel

For Israel, the Priesthood, the Sanctuary, the Sacrifices and the Festivals, were needed to prepare them for the coming of their Messiah, who would be a High Priest of the order of Melchizedek, operate in the heavenly Sanctuary where He would offer a superior sacrifice in accordance with a pre-ordained timetable to inaugurate a superior covenant. This book seeks to set forth the glory of the Lord Jesus as He fulfilled in every detail that which was prefigured by the priestly culture of Israel.

309 pages: Published by Vine Press, Newport (U.K.) (2013) ISBN: 9781904192596

Jesus of Nazareth: More than just a Messiah

This book offers Biblical evidence in support of the deity of the Lord Jesus in the hope that some will find it helpful in repelling the arguments of those who wish to diminish the One who died for the salvation of sinners. In addition, it is designed to strengthen the appreciation of the greatness of our Saviour:

93 pages: Published by Gospel Folio Press, Port Colborne (2011) ISBN: 9781926765556

The Feast of Dedication (Hanukkah)

Hanukkah had its birth during the Maccabean uprising. However, Bryan references other times of dedication in the Scriptures also. For example, at the building of the Temple during Solomon's reign and the rebuilding of the Temple when a group of exiles returned from Babylon.

He also looks at the 'abomination of desolation' that fuelled the Maccabean uprising and how it was used the Messiah to point to future events that will ultimately lead to a national dedication.

54 pages: Published by Vine Press, Newport (U.K.) (2013)
ISBN:9781904192541

12 Reasons Why I Believe Jesus was crucified on the Mount of Olives

This is a Biblical study demonstrating that the Law dictated by God required that all sacrifices had to take place to the east of the Sanctuary, and the since the Bible declares that the death of Jesus was a sacrifice for sin, then it had to take place to the east of the Temple, hence on the Mount of Olives.

This title traces the journey of the Saviour to the place of execution where the requirements of the Torah were met and prophecy fulfilled.

42 pages: Published by Vine Press, Newport (U.K.) (2014) ISBN: 9781904192701

63027207R00057

Made in the USA
Charleston, SC
26 October 2016